CYNTHIA NIMS

ILLUSTRATED BY DON BARNETT

WestWinds Press®

This book is dedicated to my husband, Bob Burns,

in gratitude for all that he brings to my life.

I could hope for no better partner.

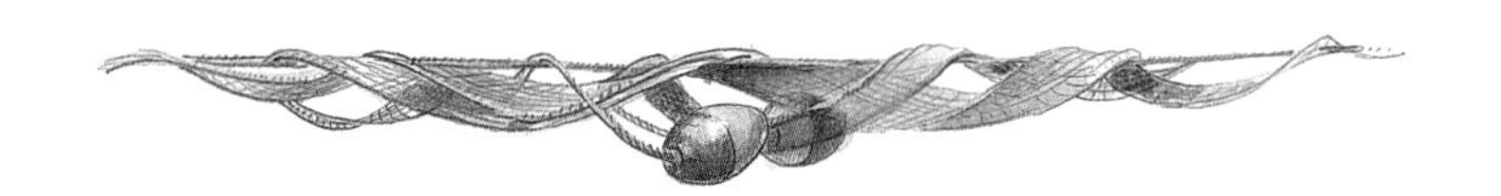

Published by WestWinds Press®
An imprint of Graphic Arts Center Publishing Company
P.O. Box 10306, Portland, Oregon 97296-0306
503-266-2402; www.gacpc.com

Library of Congress Cataloging-in-Publication Data:

Nims, Cynthia C.
Salmon / Cynthia Nims ; illustrated by Don Barnett.
p. cm. — (Northwest homegrown cookbook series)
Includes index.
ISBN 1-55868-861-7 (softbound)
1. Cookery (Salmon) 2. Salmon. I. Title. II. Series.
TX804.N55 2004
641.6'58—dc22 2004025523

President: Charles M. Hopkins
Associate Publisher: Douglas A. Pfeiffer
Editorial Staff: Timothy W. Frew, Tricia Brown, Kathy Howard, Jean Andrews, Jean Bond-Slaughter
Production Staff: Richard L. Owsiany, Susan Dupere
Editor: Ellen Wheat
Designer: Elizabeth Watson

Printed in the United States of America

Mention of the Pacific Northwest evokes powerful imagery, from the region's rugged ocean coast to massive mountain peaks, dense forests, and lush valleys, and to the rolling hills beyond. This topography along with dynamic Pacific weather patterns create the climate that, in turn, drives our seasonal rhythms—indeed, four distinct seasons. From the damp, mild coastal areas to the more extreme arid land east of the Cascade Mountains, the Northwest boasts a range of growing regions that yield a boggling array of foods. The Northwest—from Alaska and British Columbia to Washington, Idaho, Oregon, and Northern California—is a top national producer of apples, lentils, hops, hazelnuts, plums, peppermint, sweet onions, potatoes, and many types of berries. The ocean, bays, and rivers supply the region with a broad selection of fish and shellfish, and rain-soaked foothills give us prized wild mushrooms.

For the Northwest cook, this wealth of ingredients means ready access to mouth-watering edibles such as morels and asparagus with halibut in the spring, rich salmon with peaches and raspberries during summer, delicious pears, chanterelles, and cranberries harvested in the fall, and plump oysters and mussels in winter.

The distinctive bounty of our regional foods makes for a culinary landscape that is as compelling as the natural landscape. This series of *Northwest Homegrown Cookbooks* shines the spotlight on those individual foods that flourish seasonally in this place that I call home. Savor this taste of the Northwest.

ACKNOWLEDGMENTS

Research for this book came with some fascinating excursions to learn more about salmon in its natural territory. Many thanks to Kwik'pak, which made my trip to the Yukon River in Alaska possible, and to Marti Castle-Bickford, Deborah Vo, Jac Gadwill, and everyone in and around the village of Emmonak who made that adventure such a treat and an eye-opener.

Thanks to my great friend (and great photographer) Scott Wellsandt for this book's author photograph taken on the Yukon River (and for the author photos in *Wild Mushrooms* and *Stone Fruit* as well). He's a terrific travel companion and not a bad cribbage player either.

My week at King Pacific Lodge was amazing, not only a stellar chance to experience sportfishing for salmon, but another valued opportunity to learn about the life cycle of salmon and local Native traditions surrounding the great fish. Thanks to lodge manager Ken Beatty and all the guides there who shared so much knowledge of the region, and to chef Jonathan Chovancek who works wonders in that remote paradise.

My seafood mentor, Peter Redmayne, again generously shared expertise and guidance in my work on this project. Other seafood gurus, including Jon Rowley and Rick Cavanaugh, shared insights on the great Northwest fish.

Thanks, too, to Tom Quinn, professor in the School of Aquatic and Fishery Sciences at the University of Washington; to Lee Hoines, with the Washington State Department of Fish and Wildlife; to Grant Snell, general manager of the British Columbia Salmon Marketing Council; and to Janet Anderberg, food safety advisor for the Washington State Department of Health.

Leora Bloom was an indispensable help on this project, from editing to research to recipe testing. The recipe-testing team worked wonders again; my sincere thanks to Michael Amend, Jeff Ashley, Tim Kehrli, Katherine Kehrli, Barbara Nims, Ed Silver, and Susan Volland for all their help fine-tuning the recipes.

CONTENTS

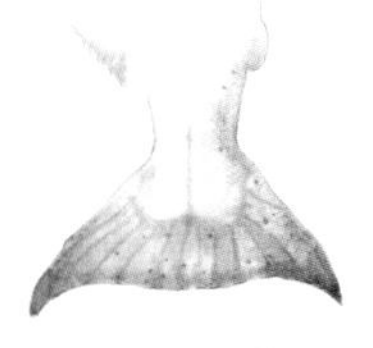

Appetizers 49

Main Courses 65

Cooking Northwest Wild Salmon 86

The Story of Northwest Salmon

Introduction

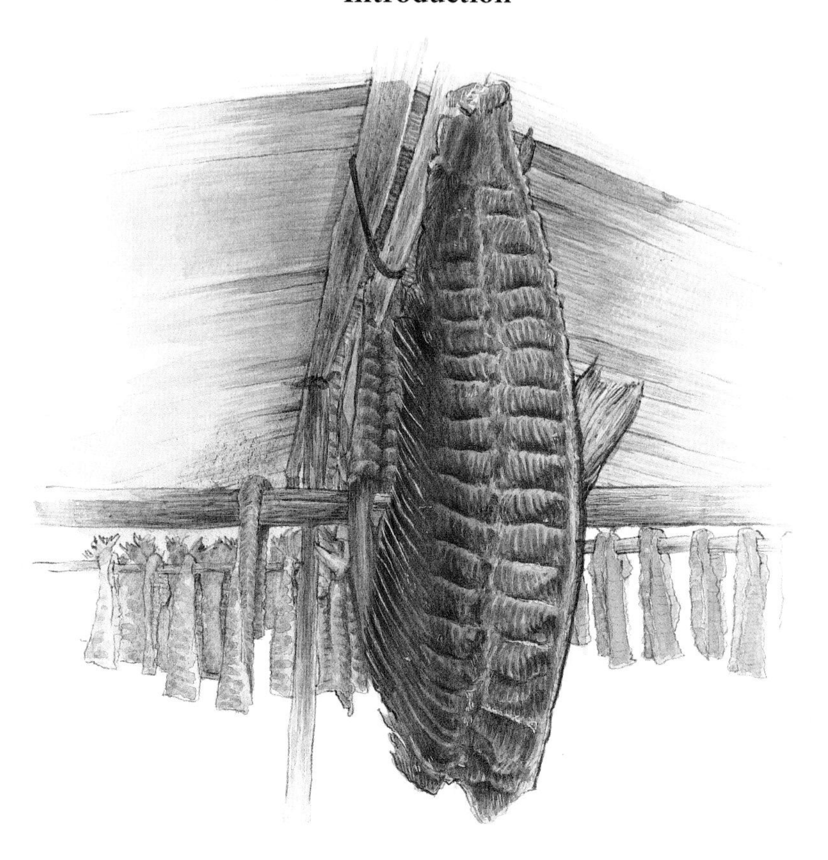

Majestic. If there is any Northwest food that conjures up such an adjective—the dignity, splendor, greatness, and regal character that it conveys—surely it is the salmon.

All walks of life appreciate the salmon. Bald eagles swoop down from perches high in cedar trees to make precision hits on the salmon with their barbed talons. Native populations have been harvesting and preserving the fish for centuries. Seals see salmon caught in gill nets as their own personal buffet. And the rest of us revel in the first bite of a just-grilled piece of the glorious fish.

Northwest Natives have long revered the salmon, among the most sustaining foods available to them. Tribes throughout the Pacific Coast have a variety of traditions and taboos surrounding Pacific salmon, reflecting the vital role the fish plays in their lives. The Quinault Indians of Washington state, for instance, have a tribal legend that the Salmon People were a powerful tribe that lived in the ocean and traveled in invisible canoes. Upon the first harvest of salmon each spring, the Quinault, like many tribes, honor the fish with celebration and ceremony, which includes returning to the sea the bones left from eating the first salmon as a sign of respect, so that the Salmon People will return again the next year.

I had the privilege of being able to visit some fish camps along the Yukon River in Alaska, near where this roughly 2,000-mile-long river spills into the Bering Sea. There were often three generations present at the camps, elders quietly watching the activities and speaking in their native Yup'ik tongue, while youngsters learned the craft by watching their parents tend nets and cut the fish for drying. One of the most awe-inspiring elements was realizing that what I was witnessing represented something timeless, with a deep connection to the earliest days of human survival in the Pacific Northwest.

When Meriwether Lewis and William Clark made their way down the mighty Columbia River to the Pacific, it must have been immeasurably clear that they had come upon a region of great bounty. In October 1805, Clark reported in his journal: "This river is remarkably clear and crouded with salmon in maney places. . . . Salmon may be seen at the depth of 15 or 20 feet. . . . The number . . . is incrediable to say." And on November 11, 1805, Clark noted: "We purchased of the Indians 13 red charr [believed to be sockeye salmon] which we found to be an excellent fish."

An excellent fish indeed. Beautiful in its cloak of iridescent silver with varying hues of blue and green, the distinctive salmon holds an honored place among this region's culinary traditions. The fish feeds us body and soul in this part of the world.

The Pacific Salmon Life Cycle: An Anadromous Journey

Pacific salmon are anadromous fish, which means that they spend part—sometimes most—of their lives in salt water but swim into freshwater rivers to spawn. A salmon begins its life typically in the spring to early summer with about 2,000 to 5,000 siblings, depending on the species and the age of the egg-laying female. The fish eggs hatch in the rocky shallows of river systems from the far north of Alaska to Southern California. After the newborn fish have consumed the nutrients from their yolk sac, the tiny fry feed on aquatic insects and zooplankton in their freshwater birth river, nourishing themselves for growth that will prepare them for the journey downstream toward their new salty ocean home. They may, depending on the species, make their way directly out to the ocean (in a matter of hours, for some pink salmon) or perhaps linger in freshwater rivers or lakes for a year or two before heading to sea.

Once in the vast reaches of the open ocean, salmon may cover a lot of territory throughout the Pacific, hundreds of miles in many cases, all the while trying to avoid predators such as seals, sharks, and whales. The fish bulk up on larval crab, shrimp, and various crustaceans, preparing for the return journey home that awaits.

When salmon reach maturity—for some as little as one year or less, others five years or longer—they begin their trip home to spawn. It defies human comprehension, but despite all the miles a salmon covers during its life, it is able to pinpoint not only the river where it was spawned, but the spot along the river where it hatched. The voyage upstream typically begins in the late summer or fall. Along the way they'll be preyed upon by humans, otters, bears, and eagles, among others. The length of the trip can be substantial: some fish travel to remote tributaries of the Yukon River, and others climb as much as 7,000 feet in elevation to reach their Idaho spawning ground. Salmon can swim at a surprisingly good clip, about 20 to 30 miles a day—and remember that's upstream against the flow of water tumbling down toward the ocean.

As salmon approach spawning time, their flesh begins to degrade. Once the fish move from salt water back to fresh, they cease feeding, fueled only by the fat they have stored in their flesh. This is why a fish caught near the mouth of a long river, such as the Columbia or Yukon, will be richer and more tasty, because their fuel tank is full of flavor-enhancing fat.

Once in their natal spawning ground, females dig into the gravel riverbed with their tails to make a nest, or "redd," and deposit their eggs. A male that she has selected fertilizes the eggs with a cloud of milt, and then he will begin to die. The females then use their tails to gently bury the eggs to slumber and incubate. Gestation varies with the species and the water conditions (temperature, mostly), and can range from about seven weeks to as long as four or five months. After this reproductive ritual, the female Pacific salmon will guard her redd for about one to three weeks before dying, completing the circle of this glorious fish's life.

Salmon are robust species. Few creatures on the planet have only one opportunity to reproduce. Only four or five of the thousands of eggs deposited by each female will be represented by returning adults to spawn. The percentage of survival seems very low, but each pair of fish is more than replacing itself in the next generation.

Our Native Pacific Salmon Species

True to its regional roots, this book addresses the wild, native salmon species of the Pacific Northwest. Salmon are in the large salmonid family of fish, which includes trout, Dolly Varden, and arctic char. Wild salmon of the Northwest share the same genus, *Oncorhynchus*, which is from the Greek for "hook" and "nose," referring to the distinctive downward bend that the tip of the male salmon's nose takes at spawning time. There are five key species of salmon in the Northwest, each with different characteristics of color, size, richness, and abundance.

King salmon (*Oncorhynchus tshawytscha*), also known as Chinook or tyee, is the largest of all Pacific salmon, averaging about 20 pounds, though specimens above 40 pounds are not uncommon. A lucky

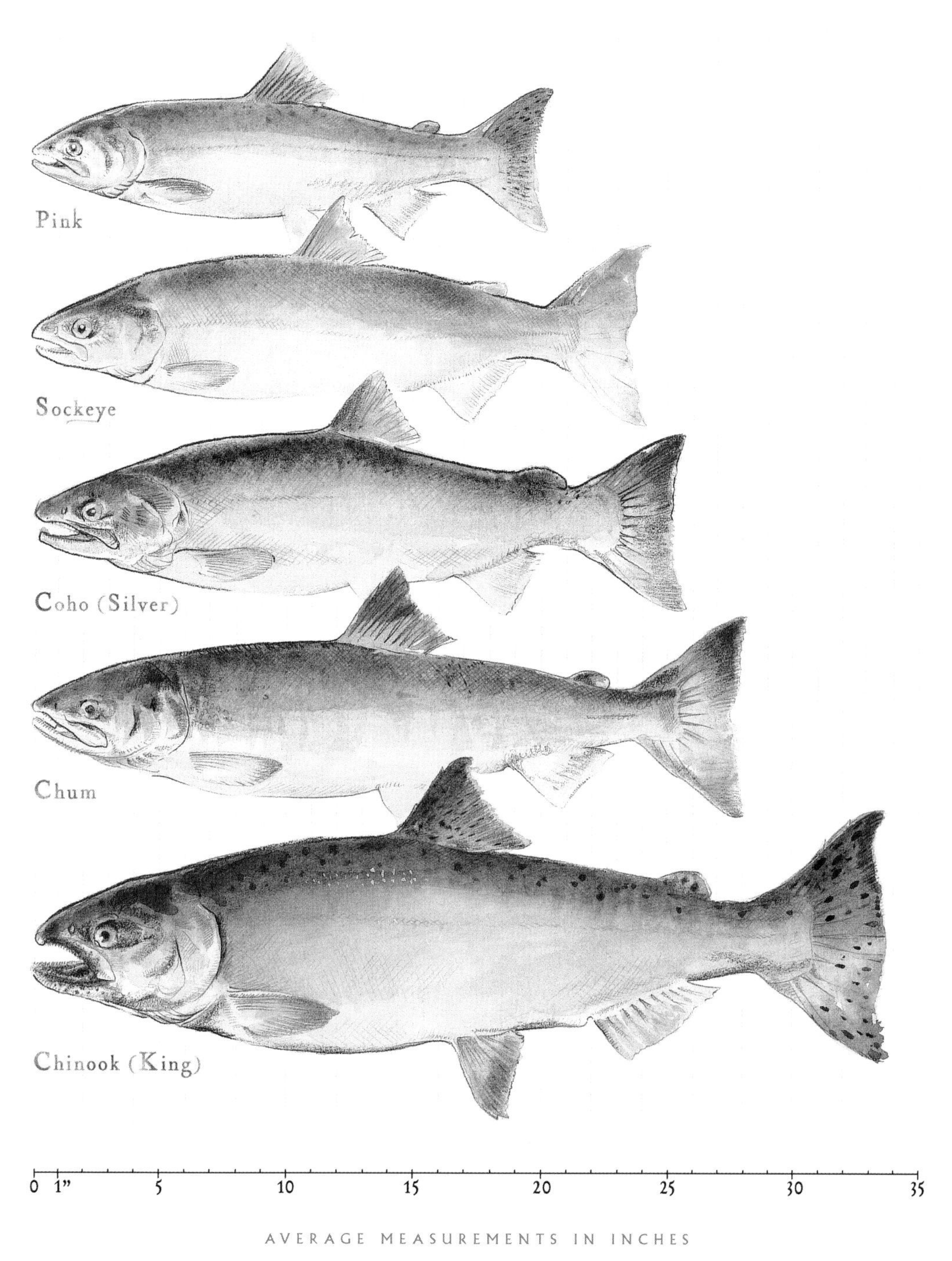

AVERAGE MEASUREMENTS IN INCHES

sportfisher on Alaska's Kenai River landed a 97-pound king, which is the world record to beat among anglers; the record commercial catch is an amazing 126 pounds. The flesh of king salmon has a moderately pronounced pink-orange hue and a high level of fat, which contributes to the distinctive rich flavor of the fish. An important commercial species, king salmon landings are a small percentage of total salmon harvest but demand brings top dollar. King is the only salmon for which Washington, Oregon, California, and British Columbia together harvest more poundage than Alaska. For all other salmon species, Alaska's catch far exceeds the combined harvest from the rest of the Pacific Coast.

King salmon usually spend three or four years in the ocean before returning to their natal streams to spawn. The ocean range of king salmon is among the greatest of all the Pacific species, from Alaska down to Southern California. The season for kings is rather long as well, from mid spring into the fall along many parts of the Pacific Coast. There is even a winter troll fishery in southeast Alaska, and Columbia River spring king salmon are fished as early as February. The fish have green- to blue-silver backs with silver-to-white flanks and black spots on their tails, plus black gums, a most distinctive characteristic.

Also known as red salmon, sockeye salmon (*Oncorhynchus nerka*) sport the most deeply colored flesh of all salmon, a near crimson orange-red. The fat level is a bit lower than that of king salmon, so the fish is flavorful but not quite as rich. Sockeye harvest is significant, both in poundage and in dollar value, making it the most commercially valuable Pacific salmon. The average weight of sockeye salmon is five to seven pounds. Japan is the most important market for sockeye, where its deep red color is particularly prized. Sockeye often spend a few years in freshwater (primarily in rivers

A Salmon by Any Other Color: The wild salmon's diet of krill and other small crustaceans is packed with carotenoids, which contributes the red-orange color of the fish's flesh. Different species have slightly varying diets and assimilate carotenoids differently, which results in the spectrum of colors found among the chum, sockeye, king, coho, and pink salmon. And within a species, the specific colors can vary in fish from one region to another, in tandem with changes in the fish's diet.

In the case of king salmon, however, some fish are simply not genetically coded with the capacity to create color in their flesh, which remains a sort of off-white. Aside from color, these fish are no different from other king salmon—the flavor and texture are the same, they simply exhibit a cosmetic color variation. You will occasionally see these fish at stores and on menus, called "white" or "ivory" king salmon.

headed by lakes), before going out to sea for a few years. The fish have a deep blue-green back (thus one nickname, bluebacks), silver sides, and a white belly. Spawning adult sockeye turn bright red, with a greenish head, unique among salmon. The sockeye salmon's range extends south to the Columbia River. Landlocked sockeye that live their whole lives in freshwater lakes are known as kokanee and are a valued sport fish.

Coho, or silver, salmon (*Oncorhynchus kisutch*) have still less fat levels, so the flavor is a bit less pronounced than king or sockeye, but still well regarded. The color of the flesh is classic "salmon," much like that of kings. The average size of coho salmon is six to eight pounds. Coho fry will spend up to a year in rivers before heading out to sea, where they'll spend another year or two before returning to freshwater. These fish have metallic-blue backs, silvery sides, and white belly coloring. Coho salmon make their way as far south as Mendocino, California.

Sometimes referred to by the name keta, chum salmon (*Oncorhynchus keta*) also has a less common nickname of "fall salmon," which hints at the fact that this fish's harvest comes in late summer/early fall while many other salmon peak in early to mid summer. Another nickname is "dog salmon," which in part reflects the oversized front teeth that develop in males during spawning. Paler in flesh and lower in fat than most other salmon, the chum is delicately flavored and averages about eight pounds. These fish migrate to salt water shortly after birth, where they'll stay for a few years before returning to rivers to spawn. Chum are primarily found in Washington waters and

northward. Their coloring is metallic blue-green on top, silvery-white on the sides.

Pink salmon (*Oncorhynchus gorbuscha*) is the smallest of the Pacific salmon, sometimes known as "humpies" because of the pronounced hump that develops on males shortly before spawning. Pinks consistently represent the largest catch of Pacific salmon, a significant mainstay for the fishing industry. The softly colored flesh is the leanest of all salmon, not as prized for gourmet culinary treatment but a good catch nonetheless, and available typically at bargain prices. The majority of pink salmon, which average less than four pounds, are canned. The fish often migrate directly to salt water after hatching and spend about two years at sea before returning to spawn. Pink salmon are metallic blue-green above and silvery below.

Of Pacific salmon kin, the closest relatives are steelhead and rainbow trout (*Oncorhynchus mykiss*) and cutthroat trout (*Oncorhynchus clarki*, named in honor of William Clark from the Lewis and Clark expedition, which includes many subspecies). Steelhead and rainbows are the same fish, though the latter lives its full life only in freshwater, while the former is an anadromous fish, making the journey to salt water and back like salmon do (though steelhead don't necessarily die after spawning). The steelhead was adopted as the state fish by the Washington legislature in 1969. In the same family, but different genus, are such fish as arctic char (*Salvelinus alpinus*), brook trout (*Salvelinus fontinalis*) and many other kinds of trout, as well as Atlantic salmon (*Salmo salar*). Numbers of wild Atlantic salmon are in critical decline, but this fish is available worldwide because the species is most commonly raised in salmon farming operations.

Salmon Fishing in the Northwest

Natives have been harvesting salmon for countless generations. In broad bays and rivers, nets suspended between canoes captured fish, and they trolled for salmon from canoes, the line (made of braided hair) and hook (of wood and bone) dangling in the water from behind. In rushing, tumbling waters farther upriver, Natives built platforms out over the turbulent river, using large dipnets to skillfully scoop up the leaping salmon working their way up to spawning grounds. During a recent visit to King Pacific Lodge in British Columbia, I saw while hiking evidence of ancient weirs built by the local Tsimshian Indians, which served to corral salmon in shallow bays, making harvest easier for their subsistence needs.

After the arrival of European settlers, the business of catching salmon began. Hapgood, Hume & Co. was the first cannery on record, which started operation—albeit limited and rather crude—on the Sacramento River in 1864. A third-generation fisherman, William Hume came to California from Maine, along with friend Andrew Hapgood, who had trained as a tinsmith and had some experience canning lobster back home. The Sacramento River proved to be not as reliable a salmon source as hoped, and in 1866 the team opened their second cannery on the Columbia River at Eagle Cliff, Washington. There they put up 4,000 cases (each with 48 one-pound cans) in their first year, and production leapt to 18,000 cases the following year. With not yet much market for the canned salmon in the area, much of this product went to Australia until demand grew locally.

The industry flourished in coming years. In British Columbia, the first salmon cannery was established on the Fraser River in the 1870s, and in a matter of decades many dozens of canneries operated in the region. In 1878 the North Pacific Packing and Trading Company established a salmon cannery in Klawock, Alaska, said to be the first in the territory, and helped spawn the commercial salmon industry in the Far North.

Ten years after opening, the Hapgood, Hume & Co. cannery on the Columbia River packed 450,000 cases of salmon. In 1893,

R. D. Hume (who I believe was a brother of William Hume) wrote of the lumbermen, builders, boatmen, and others who supported the salmon canneries: "We find all trades and professions plunging to get a whack at this new El Dorado, all seeking a fortune to be made from the capture of the scaly beauties. What a mine of wealth, that even all who might plunge might be enriched."

A map published in the *New York Commercial* newspaper in April 1901 shows extraordinary detail across approximately 3,500 nautical miles that stretch from San Francisco to Kuskokwim Bay on the Bering Sea in Alaska, indicating locations of over 200 salmon canneries at that time. Each cannery is listed by name, location, and sales agent. Data on the Columbia River, Sacramento River, "Outside" rivers, Puget Sound, British Columbia, and Alaska—from inception of the industry in 1866 through 1900—accounts for a whopping 39,749,770 *cases* of salmon cans produced.

By the mid 1900s, less than scrupulous cannery owners seemed to consider Alaska's supply of salmon as something of a free-for-all, seriously depleting stocks. Residents of the then-territory couldn't stand quietly by to allow the decimation of such a precious resource. This frustration was one of many considerations that helped propel them toward statehood, their constitution adopting wording to require mindful preservation of all natural resources, including the great salmon.

Today, Alaska is by far the largest source of wild Pacific salmon, accounting for about 85 percent of the total commercial catch on the west coast of North America. The size of the resource is hard to imagine. In recent years, the annual harvest of salmon in Alaska waters has been well over 500 million pounds—as high as near one billion pounds in 1995 and 1996, with lows in the 140-million-pound range in the early 1970s. Washington, Oregon, California, and British Columbia together represent a commercial harvest of about 100 million pounds each year.

There are three key methods by which salmon are caught. Trolling accounts for the smallest percentage of salmon harvest—about 10 percent—but produces fish that are generally of the highest value, pound for pound. King and coho make up the bulk of salmon in troll fisheries. Trolling is the standard method for ocean fishing, while nets are more commonly used for fishing in rivers and closer to shore. Hook-and-line fishing on a large scale, boats troll by dragging a number of weighted lines behind the boat, each with lures or baited hooks. It's a very hands-on method, as each fish much be individually removed from its hook, cleaned, and packed on ice right away to maintain that maximum of quality. Smaller boats will make day-trips,

returning to port each evening, while larger boats may stay out for a matter of days. In the smaller Washington, Oregon, California, and British Columbia fisheries, trolling generally accounts for the largest portion of their harvest.

A large number of salmon are caught by gill net, a large net in which the fish become tangled by their gills, the size of the net mesh chosen to target certain fish and allow smaller fish to swim through. The net is set vertically in the water in the estimated path of the salmon, secured at one end with a buoy, attached to the boat at the other. In drift gillnetting, the weighted net is dragged behind the boat, and in setnetting the net is attached between fixed supports. The net is periodically lifted to the boat deck to remove the fish individually.

Purse seining is the third of the primary salmon fishing methods and the one that accounts for the largest volume of harvest. A fine-mesh heavy net is dropped from the purse seiner into the water, the net weighted at the bottom to draw it squarely down. The net is secured at its outer edge by a small skiff, which draws the net in a large circle around a school of salmon, and joins the two ends of the net at the larger boat. The bottom of the net is then drawn closed as with the strings of a purse, and the whole load lifted up onto the boat and transferred to the hold.

Sustainable Wild Salmon

Sustainability of our food sources is a hot topic lately, and rightfully so. This is particularly true in the world of seafood, the category of food for which we rely more on wild, natural stocks than any other.

The Marine Stewardship Council studies targeted fishery practices around the world to determine their level of sustainability and educate the public about issues surrounding the future of wild seafood supplies. The MSC has certified all five species of Pacific salmon harvested in Alaska waters as sustainable. Conservative fishery management is part of what helps make the future of Pacific salmon so bright. I've seen the Alaska Department of Fish and Game at work in salmon fishing territory in two different areas—on Kodiak Island and on the Yukon River—keeping close tabs on the numbers of salmon heading into river systems. Known as "escapements," these fish returning to their natal spawning grounds are the ultimate goal of fishery management, assuring that sufficient salmon return to spawn for healthy stocks in seasons to come. On inhabited rivers, subsistence fishing needs are an important priority, and on river systems that continue into Canada, enough fish must pass also for their allotment. It is an elaborate but well-managed system.

As I finish work on this book, both California (troll-caught king) and British Columbia (all species, but special emphasis on sockeye) were pursuing MSC certification for their salmon fisheries. The process includes extensive review of the status of the fish stocks, study of effects the fishery has on the surrounding ecosystem, and assessment of the effectiveness of systems in place to manage the fishery. Certification can take several months or a few years, depending on the complexity of the fishery and the time needed for a thorough evaluation.

About the Recipes

Salmon brings a good deal of flavor and character to any recipe. Typically, Northwest cooks prefer to keep things simple with our native wild salmon, allowing the distinctive qualities of the fish to shine through. Basic grilled salmon is a regional classic, the earthy-aromatic elements of outdoor grilling melding beautifully with the richness of the fish—add a handful of wood chips to the coals and the marriage is even more tasty. But in this cookbook you'll find a wide range of salmon recipes, from grilled whole salmon the way my dad used to always do it to Salmon and Sunchoke Chowder and Sesame-Crusted Salmon Steaks with Wasabi Butter.

Not all salmon are created equal. Different species (and even the same species caught in different waters at different times of the season) will have varying levels of flavor, color, moisture, and richness. In broad terms, it means that one variety of salmon may be preferable over another for some cooking methods—such as fatty king for grilling or leaner chum for steaming. But because shoppers often have only one or two options at a given time, these recipes generally do not call for a specific variety. You may, of course, use farmed salmon if that is all that is available. But very good frozen-at-sea wild salmon is available year-round, and some stores that make special efforts to source their salmon can provide you with fresh wild salmon virtually all year long as well.

Breakfast / Brunch

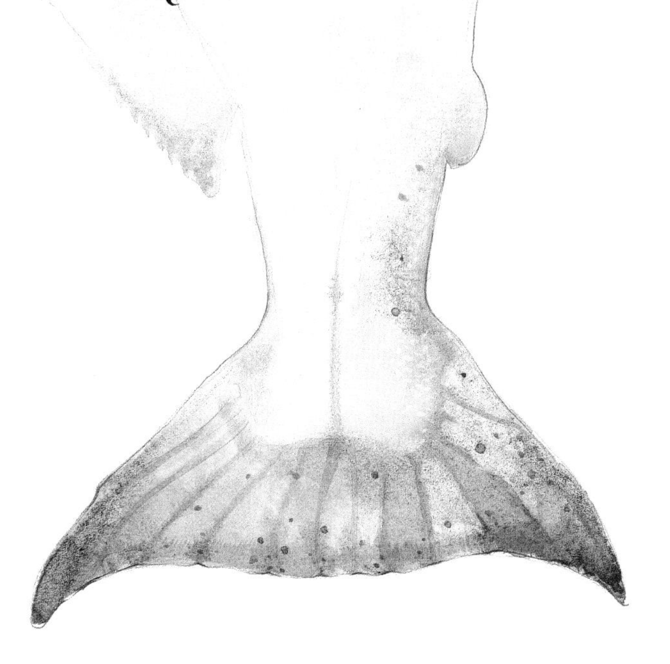

Poached Eggs on Salmon, Leek, and Potato Cakes

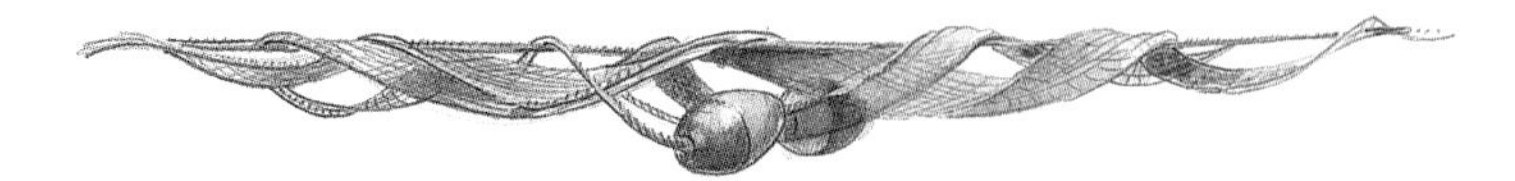

These savory salmon cakes—without the poached eggs—would also make a great side dish at dinnertime. For a more elaborate morning meal, you could top the poached eggs with hollandaise sauce and omit the sour cream.

- 1 pound russet potatoes, peeled
- 8 ounces cooked salmon, finely flaked, skin and pin bones removed (about 1 cup)
- 1 large or 2 small leeks, white and pale green parts only, split, cleaned, and sliced
- ¼ cup minced flat-leaf (Italian) parsley
- 2 tablespoons all-purpose flour
- 5 eggs
- Salt and freshly ground white or black pepper
- 2 tablespoons unsalted butter
- 2 tablespoons olive oil, more if needed
- 2 teaspoons distilled white vinegar
- Sour cream, for serving (optional)

Coarsely grate the potatoes and put them in a large bowl. Add the salmon, leek, parsley, and flour. Lightly beat 1 of the eggs in a small dish and add it to the bowl with a generous seasoning of salt and pepper. Toss well to thoroughly mix.

Heat the butter and oil in a large skillet, preferably nonstick, over medium heat. When hot, add the salmon mixture, forming 4 cakes about ½ inch thick. Cook until the bottom is nicely browned, about 6 minutes, then turn and continue cooking until tender when pierced with the tip of a knife and crisp on the outside, 6 to 8 minutes longer. Transfer the cakes to a paper-towel lined baking sheet and keep warm in a low oven while poaching the eggs.

Half-fill a deep skillet with water and add the vinegar. Bring the water to a gentle boil over medium-high heat, then carefully crack the remaining 4 eggs into the water. (To avoid scalding your knuckles, you could first crack each egg into a small bowl, then gently tip the egg from the bowl into the water.) Reduce the heat to medium and simmer gently until the egg whites are set and the yolks are still soft, 3 to 4 minutes, gently sloshing some of the water over the top of the eggs once or twice during cooking to help set the surface of the yolk. Scoop out the eggs with a slotted spoon and drain them on a plate lined with paper towels.

To serve, set the salmon cakes on individual plates, top with the poached eggs, and serve right away, with a dollop of sour cream alongside if you like.

Makes 4 servings

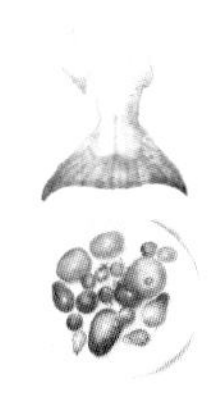

Salmon "Bacon"

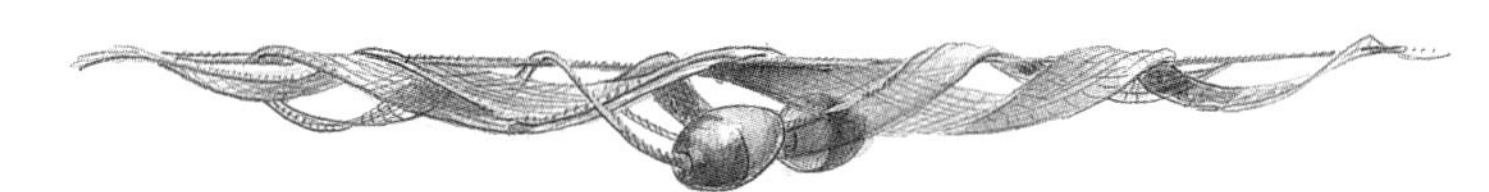

This recipe is something of a twist on smoked salmon. You brine the fish as you traditionally would (though cut in strips first) and bake the salmon rather than smoking it. It is just the thing to serve with scrambled eggs and toast for a special breakfast. Be sure to choose a thicker fillet portion of salmon, from the head end rather than the tail end, so that the slices will be of relatively even width. The salmon can be brined, drained, and dried the day before. Wrap the salmon strips in plastic and bake just before serving for best results.

3 cups warm water
¾ cup real maple syrup or honey
6 tablespoons kosher salt
2 teaspoons coarsely ground black pepper
¾ pound salmon fillet, skin and pin bones removed
1 tablespoon vegetable oil

Combine the water, maple syrup, and salt in a large shallow dish, such as a 9-by-13-inch baking dish. Stir to mix and let sit until the salt has dissolved and the brine has fully cooled, stirring occasionally, 15 to 20 minutes.

Sprinkle the pepper evenly over both sides of the salmon fillet, rubbing well with your fingers to evenly coat the fish and help it adhere. Cut the salmon fillet across into ¼-inch slices and lay them in the brine mixture, avoiding overlapping. Cover the dish with plastic wrap and refrigerate for 1 hour.

Lift the salmon strips from the brine and drain on paper towels, patting the tops with paper towel as well. Set the strips on a wire rack and air dry until the surface of the fish is no longer moist to the touch, about 45 minutes. If you have a small fan, set it up to blow gently on the salmon to speed up the drying.

Preheat the oven to 250°F. Line a large baking sheet with foil.

Lightly brush both sides of each salmon strip with the oil and lay them on the prepared baking sheet. Bake the salmon until aromatic and firm, about 45 minutes. Let sit on the pan for a few minutes, then serve.

Makes 6 to 8 servings

The Sport of Salmon

There was a lot of hubbub at the Prince Rupert, British Columbia, airport when I arrived on a Monday afternoon. I'd just landed from Vancouver and was about to make the last leg of a daylong journey to King Pacific Lodge. It had been something of a testosterone-filled flight, men of all ages converging on this north British Columbia destination for their often-annual pilgrimage to one of the province's 150 or so fishing lodges. The friendly ribbing began on the flight, with talk of the money pool they'd be fishing to win and of silly fish hats ("Which way did they go?"). It is a different type of Northwest salmon ritual, but a ritual nonetheless. I decided it was high time I get a taste of this tradition for myself.

Located on Barnard Harbour about an hour's floatplane ride from Prince Rupert, King Pacific Lodge is a spectacular spot for the sport of fishing. Within moments of setting foot on the floating resort (built on an old U.S. Army barge), the nine of us were offered the chance to jump right into activities. I opted for a quick predinner hike, which took me to nearby Cameron Cove, dropped onto the shore with my guide, Marlene. We maneuvered across the barnacle-covered shore rocks, which took us past evidence of ancient Native (or First Nations, as they are called in Canada) salmon weirs, low stone walls extending perpendicularly from the shore out into the shallow bay. Salmon would come deep into the bay at high tide and as the tide receded, would linger behind the weirs, making easy work of harvesting the fish with nets or spears.

We then ventured into the ultra-lush second-growth forest alongside a gently rushing river. In the deep moss, Marlene's eagle eye picked out the partial remains of the lower jaw bone of a chum salmon, which attains a sort of sabertooth salmon look during spawning, its jaw protruding with a grotesque show of teeth. A bear last fall must have swooped up this salmon from the river and carried it these few dozen yards into the forest to avoid competition from other bears. After making a fine meal of the salmon, the bear left the carcass at the base of a huge cedar, where it would decompose and nourish the plant life. It was fascinating to get this up-close exposure to the complete cycle of life that the Pacific salmon has.

But back to the fishing! I'd recently read that while "tyee" is considered to be a pseudonym of king salmon, in some circles the term is used specifically to designate a fish weighing 30 pounds or more. Here at the lodge, landing such a fish indeed warrants you a vibrant gold tyee pin, which quickly became the most coveted piece of jewelry on the property. Bill and Kay from Florida were the only ones in our group to go home with that prize. As for me, I think my tyee pin was carried away deep into the cold, blue water along with the tackle gear that broke from the end of my rod as I was working to reel the big guy in. I have no regrets, though. My fishing guide, Darryl, worked his magic to help me bring in a 28-pound fish that we later discovered to have white flesh dappled with soft orange, and an 18-pound male with beautifully deep red color. I also tried my hand at saltwater fly-fishing, casting the weighted line while trying to maintain my balance at the bow of a small boat, not the most graceful thing I've ever attempted. While I caught, and released, a boatload of black rockfish (aka black bass), it was a little early in the season for much hope of landing a salmon by fly. Expert fly fisher and lodge manager Ken Beatty has, to date, played king salmon as big as 30 pounds on his fly rod.

Friday we were back at the Prince Rupert airport for our return flight to Vancouver, each with our sizeable, well-packed box of flash-frozen fish (except for Bob and Joanne who chose to have their fish smoked and sent to them in Texas). As we waited in the sweltering departure lounge, the afternoon plane came in from Vancouver packed with a new bunch of folks, all with dreams of big fish in their eyes. And so the ritualistic journey to meet the glorious salmon on its own turf continues.

Salmon and Tomato Breakfast Pie

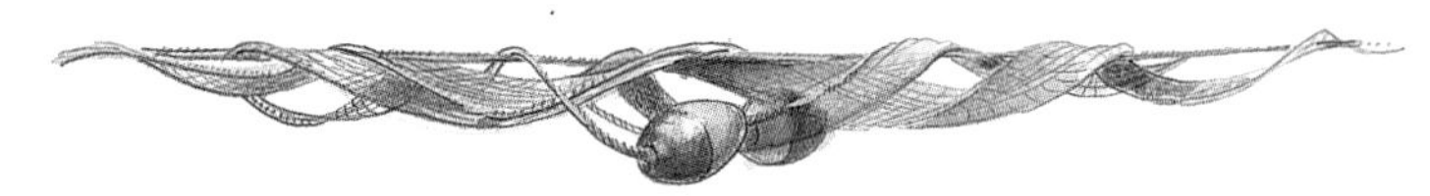

Something like a quiche, this savory chive- and thyme-speckled pie of salmon and tomatoes is bound together with eggs and a touch of cheese. It would also make for a perfect luncheon dish, with a simple green salad alongside.

3 eggs
1½ cups half-and-half
2 tablespoons minced chives
½ teaspoon thyme leaves
Salt and freshly ground white or black pepper
¾ pound cooked salmon, flaked, skin and pin bones removed (about 1½ cups)
8 ounces tomatoes, cut into ¼-inch slices (or halved, if cherry tomatoes)
½ cup grated Gruyère or Swiss cheese

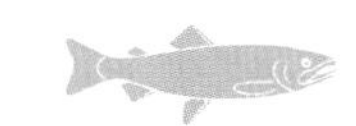

Pastry Dough

1½ cups all-purpose flour
½ teaspoon salt
½ cup unsalted butter, cut into pieces and chilled
4 to 5 tablespoons ice water, more if needed

For the pastry dough, combine the flour and salt in a food processor and pulse once to mix. Add the butter and pulse until the butter is finely chopped and the flour mixture has a coarse sandy texture. Drizzle the water into the dough 1 tablespoon at a time, again pulsing briefly a few times to just blend. It's important not to overmix the dough or it will be tough rather than flaky. The dough will not form a ball in the machine, but has the proper amount of liquid if squeezing some of the dough between your fingers feels neither dusty dry nor sticky. (Alternatively, combine the flour and salt in a large bowl and cut in the butter with a pastry cutter or two table knives until it has a coarse sandy texture. Add the water 1 tablespoon at a time and stir with a fork to mix, adding more water if needed.) Turn the dough out onto the work surface, form it into a ball, and wrap it in plastic. Refrigerate the dough for at least 30 minutes before rolling it out.

Preheat the oven to 400°F.

Roll out the chilled dough on a lightly floured surface to a roughly 12-inch circle and use it to line a 9- to 10-inch pie pan (preferably not deep-dish). Press the dough gently down the sides of the pan to be sure it is evenly covering the bottom. Using kitchen shears, trim the outer edge of the dough to a ½-inch overhang, then fold that edge under and use your fingers to flute the pastry edge. Prick the bottom of the shell with the tines of a fork, line the pastry shell with a piece of foil or parchment paper, and add pie weights or dry beans to cover the bottom. Bake the pastry shell until the edges are set, about 10 minutes. Take the pan from the oven, remove the foil and weights, and continue baking until the crust is lightly browned and the bottom no longer looks raw, 5 to 7 minutes longer. (If the bottom of the shell puffs up, re-prick the dough.) Take the crust from the oven and let cool slightly; reduce the oven temperature to 375°F.

Whisk together the eggs in a medium bowl until blended, then whisk in the half-and-half, chives, and thyme with salt and pepper to taste. Scatter the salmon evenly over the bottom of the cooled pie shell and arrange the tomatoes on top. Pour the egg mixture over the tomatoes, then sprinkle the cheese evenly over the top. Bake until the filling is set and a knife inserted in the center comes out clean, 35 to 40 minutes. Let sit on a wire rack for about 5 minutes before cutting into wedges to serve.

Makes 8 servings

Spinach and Salmon Frittata

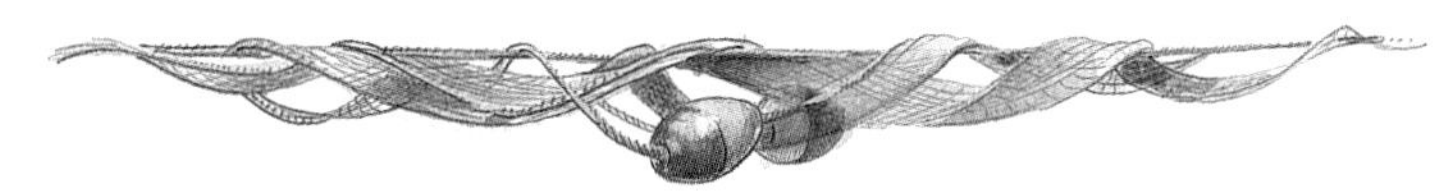

A delectable eye-opener for any morning of the week, this frittata can be streamlined by using leftover cooked salmon and bagged, prewashed spinach leaves. Serve with toast, juice, and coffee, and you're ready to meet the day.

2 tablespoons unsalted butter
8 ounces salmon fillet, skin and pin bones removed, cut into ½-inch strips
½ cup chopped shallot or onion
½ bunch spinach (about 8 ounces), rinsed, dried, and tough stems removed
8 eggs
Salt and freshly ground white or black pepper
¼ cup sliced green onions
½ cup freshly grated Parmesan cheese

Preheat the oven to 375°F.

Melt 1 tablespoon of the butter in a medium ovenproof skillet, preferably nonstick, over medium heat. Add the salmon strips and cook until nearly opaque through and just lightly browned, 1 to 2 minutes per side. Transfer the salmon to a plate and set aside. Melt the remaining 1 tablespoon of the butter in the skillet, add the shallot, and cook, stirring, until it just begins to soften, 2 to 3 minutes. Add the spinach a handful or two at a time, stirring to help it cook evenly before adding the next batch. When all of the spinach is wilted, in 2 to 3 minutes, take the skillet from the heat and spread the spinach and shallot evenly over the bottom of the skillet.

Whisk the eggs in a medium bowl until well blended, then season generously with salt and pepper. Slowly pour the eggs over the frittata filling, stirring gently to distribute some of the egg under the spinach. Break the salmon strips into bite-size pieces and lay them on the frittata in a tidy pattern. Scatter the green onions over the top, followed by an even layer of the cheese.

Return the skillet to medium heat until the base is set and the edges are beginning to firm up, about 5 minutes. Transfer the skillet to the oven and bake just until the top is set and the eggs are cooked through, 8 to 10 minutes longer. Cut the frittata into wedges and serve right away.

Makes 6 to 8 servings

Tale of Two Peppers: Not all kitchens have both white and black peppercorns on hand, but if you have two pepper grinders in the house, I'd recommend that you fill one with black and the other with white peppercorns. While the aesthetic shock of tiny dark specks of black pepper in food isn't a big concern in our home kitchens, it is nice to have white pepper on hand when you want to avoid that culinary distraction, whether on a pristine piece of fish or in fluffy scrambled eggs.

White and black peppercorns are from the same plant: the former has had the skin removed after drying, the latter leaves the skin on to darken, which contributes a slightly more pronounced flavor.

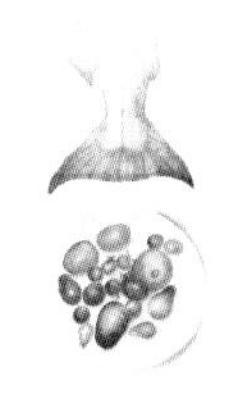

Salmon, Potato, and Sweet Onion Breakfast Bake

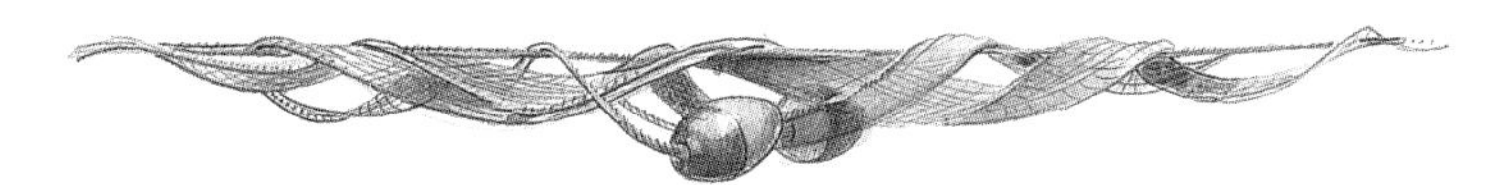

This easy recipe combines the hash brown element of sautéed onions and potatoes with eggs and the added flavor of flaked, cooked salmon. You could bake this dish the night before, let cool, and refrigerate, then simply reheat it the next morning before serving.

2 tablespoons unsalted butter
1 tablespoon vegetable oil
¾ pound red potatoes, scrubbed and cut into ¼-inch slices
Salt and freshly ground white or black pepper
½ large Walla Walla Sweet onion or 1 medium yellow onion, cut into ¼-inch slices
¾ pound cooked salmon, finely flaked, skin and pin bones removed (about 1½ cups)
6 eggs
¼ cup heavy cream or milk

Melt the butter with the oil in a large skillet over medium heat. Add the potato slices with a pinch each of salt and pepper, and cook until beginning to soften, 5 to 7 minutes, stirring often. Add the sliced onion and continue cooking until both the potatoes and onions are tender and lightly browned, 5 to 7 minutes longer.

Preheat the oven to 350°F. Generously butter a 9- to 10-inch quiche pan or other shallow baking dish.

Scatter the potato and onion mixture evenly over the bottom of the prepared quiche pan and sprinkle the flaked salmon on top. Whisk together the eggs in a medium bowl, then add the cream with a good pinch each of salt and pepper and whisk to thoroughly blend. Pour the egg mixture over the salmon, and bake until the egg is set and the edge is lightly browned, about 30 minutes.

Set aside on a wire rack for a few minutes, then cut into wedges to serve.

Makes 6 to 8 servings

Homemade Bagels with Salmon and Cream Cheese

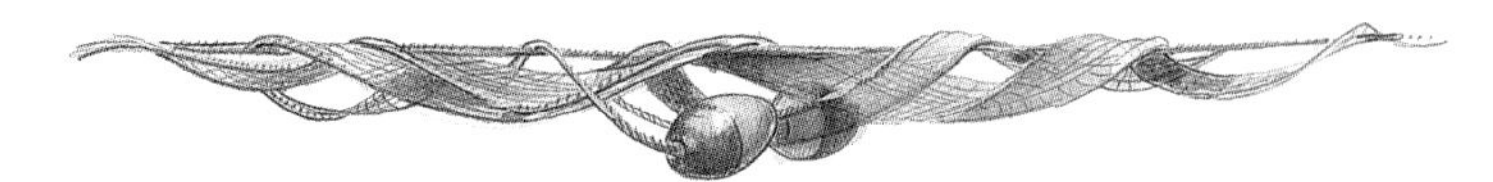

Okay, sure, you can take a shortcut and purchase the best bagels you can get your hands on for this classic brunchtime meal. Though it takes a few hours from start to finish, it's not complicated to make bagels at home, and nothing beats the flavor and aroma of just-baked bagels from your own oven.

A bagel-making DJ friend of mine told me about using malt powder, the kind you would sprinkle over ice cream or use in a malted milkshake, in place of the malt syrup, which can be tricky to find. Look for malt syrup with syrups or baking goods in well-stocked stores, or at health food stores. I've tested this recipe with both, tasty results all around. Plain cream cheese is ideal for topping the bagels, but for a little added flavor consider stirring in some minced green onion, or offer both plain and onion cream cheese to your guests.

6 to 8 ounces Gin- and Juniper-Cured Salmon (page 61) or cold-smoked salmon, cut into very thin slices
8 ounces cream cheese, at room temperature
¼ large red onion, thinly sliced
1 small tomato, thinly sliced
¼ cup capers

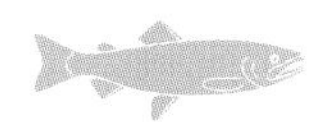

Bagels

1½ cups warm water (about 110°F)
2 tablespoons malt syrup or malt powder
2 teaspoons active dry yeast
4½ cups all-purpose flour, more if needed
2 teaspoons salt

For the bagels, put the warm water in a small bowl and quickly stir in 1 tablespoon of the malt syrup to mix. Sprinkle the yeast over, stir to mix, and set aside until dissolved and bubbly, about 5 minutes. Put the flour in the bowl of a mixer, add the salt, and stir to mix. Make a well in the center of the flour and add the proofed yeast mixture. Mix with the paddle attachment to form a smooth dough, adding a bit more flour if the dough is sticky.

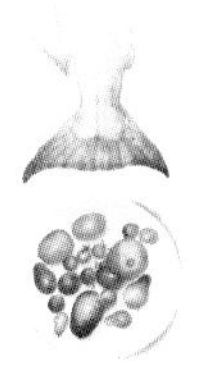

Switch to the hook attachment and knead the dough until satiny, about 5 minutes. You may mix the dough by hand as well, in a large bowl with a heavy wooden spoon, then knead the dough on a lightly floured work surface for about 5 minutes.

Form the dough into a ball, cover with a kitchen towel, and set aside in a warm spot to rise until doubled in bulk. Punch down the dough and cut it into 12 even portions (about 3 ounces each). Use your hands to roll 1 piece of the dough to a cylinder about 12 inches long. Draw the ends together and pinch them to seal well, then form a circle about 4 inches across. Set the bagel on a lightly oiled baking sheet and continue with the remaining dough. When all the bagels have been formed, cover them with a kitchen towel and set aside in a warm spot to rise by about half, 30 to 40 minutes.

Preheat the oven to 375°F. Generously dust 2 baking sheets with cornmeal.

Fill a large, deep sauté pan or broad pot with 2 to 3 inches of water. Add the remaining 1 tablespoon of the malt syrup and bring to a boil over high heat. Reduce the heat to medium and add 2 or 3 of the bagels to the water; don't crowd, so that the bagels touch as little as possible to avoid sticking. Handle the risen bagels gently when transferring them to the water to avoid deflating them. Simmer the bagels for about 30 seconds and use a slotted spoon to carefully turn them over; continue cooking until lightly firm on the surface and their shape is set, about 30 seconds longer. Lift the bagels out with a large slotted spoon and drain on a wire rack. When you have simmered 6 bagels, arrange them on one of the baking sheets and bake until nicely browned, about 20 minutes. Meanwhile, continue simmering the remaining bagels and bake the second sheet after the first batch is out of the oven. (I prefer baking one sheet at a time for the most even results; you may bake both at the same time, but switch the trays on the two oven shelves halfway through for best results.) Let the bagels cool on a wire rack and serve slightly warm or at room temperature.

To serve, slice the bagels in half and pass the toppings separately for guests to pile on their bagels to taste.

Makes 12 servings

Kedgeree

Made traditionally with smoked haddock (a type of cod), this classic English breakfast recipe takes well to a Northwest twist with salmon. Feel free to use just fresh or smoked salmon, if you prefer, rather than the fresh-and-smoked combination.

4 eggs
2 tablespoons olive oil
⅓ cup sliced green onion
2 teaspoons curry powder (mild or hot), more to taste
3 cups cooked long grain white rice
8 ounces fresh, cooked salmon, flaked, skin and pin bones removed (about 1 cup)
1 cup coarsely chopped hot-smoked salmon, skin and pin bones removed
¼ cup salmon stock (page 37) or water, more if needed
2 tablespoons minced flat-leaf (Italian) parsley
Salt and freshly ground white or black pepper

Put the eggs in a medium saucepan with enough cold water to cover them by about 1 inch. Put the pan over high heat and bring to a boil, then reduce the heat to medium-high and set the timer for 10 minutes. Drain the eggs and run cold water over them for a few minutes to stop the cooking and help cool the eggs quickly (which also helps make them easier to peel). Peel the eggs. Quarter 1 of the eggs for garnish and coarsely chop the remaining 3 eggs.

Heat the olive oil in a large skillet over medium heat. Add the green onion and toss for about 30 seconds, then add the curry powder and stir until it evenly coats the green onion and smells quite aromatic, about 1 minute. Add the cooked rice and both types of salmon and cook, stirring often to evenly mix, then drizzle the stock over and cook until the ingredients are heated through, 3 to 5 minutes. If the mixture still seems a bit dry, add another few teaspoons or so of stock or water.

Stir the chopped egg and parsley into the kedgeree and season to taste with salt and pepper. Spoon the kedgeree onto individual plates, top with a wedge of hard-boiled egg, and serve.

Makes 4 servings

Soups, Salads, and Sandwiches

Salmon and Sunchoke Chowder

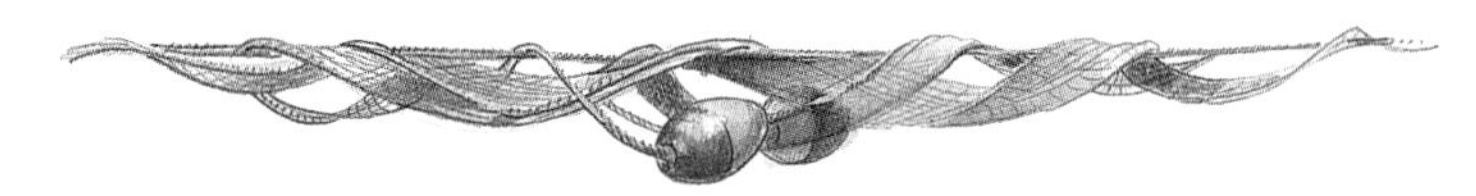

The sunchoke (also known as Jerusalem artichoke) is an uncommon but delicious tuber with a nutty-earthy-sweet flavor reminiscent of an artichoke heart, hence that part of its name. You could substitute parsnips or potatoes, if you're unable to find sunchokes. Parsnips should be peeled and halved, with the tough central core trimmed away before dicing.

¾ pound sunchokes
3 tablespoons unsalted butter
½ medium onion, finely chopped
1 large carrot, cut into ½-inch dice
1 large leek, white and pale green parts only, split, cleaned, and thinly sliced
Salt and freshly ground white or black pepper
4 cups salmon stock (page 37) or fish stock
2 cups half-and-half
1 pound salmon fillet, skin and pin bones removed
½ teaspoon minced thyme

Use the back edge of a small knife or a vegetable peeler to scrape away the thin skin from the sunchokes, dropping them into a bowl of water as you're done to help reduce discoloration. When all the sunchokes have been peeled, drain them well and cut them into roughly ½-inch dice.

Melt the butter in a large saucepan over medium heat. Add the sunchokes, onion, carrot, leek, and a pinch each of salt and pepper. Sauté, stirring occasionally, until the vegetables begin to soften, 8 to 10 minutes (the vegetables shouldn't brown; reduce the heat if needed). Add the salmon stock and half-and-half. Bring the liquid just to a boil over medium-high heat, then reduce the heat to medium-low and simmer until the vegetables are fully tender, about 30 minutes.

Cut the salmon fillet into ½-inch dice and add it to the chowder with the thyme. Simmer, stirring very gently once or twice, just until the salmon is cooked through, 2 to 3 minutes. Taste the chowder for seasoning, adding more salt or pepper to taste. Ladle the chowder into individual bowls and serve right away.

Makes 4 to 6 servings

Asparagus Soup with Salmon

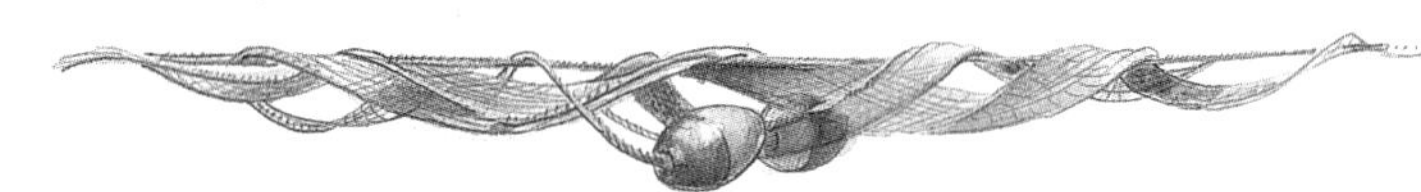

This is a very pretty soup, the soft springtime green of the asparagus purée speckled with flakes of pink salmon. It would also be tasty served chilled. An optional garnish is toasted baguette slices spread with a thin layer of fresh, mild goat cheese and topped with a bit of the flaked salmon.

2 tablespoons unsalted butter
1½ cups chopped onion
Salt and freshly ground white or black pepper
3 cups salmon stock (page 37), fish stock, or mild chicken stock
¾ pound salmon fillet, skin and pin bones removed
1½ pounds asparagus, trimmed and coarsely chopped
1 cup half-and-half

Melt the butter in a medium saucepan over medium heat. Add the onion with a good pinch each of salt and pepper, and cook, stirring occasionally, until tender and aromatic, 3 to 5 minutes. Add the stock and bring just to a boil. While the stock is heating, cut the salmon fillet into large pieces about 3 inches square. Gently lower the salmon pieces into the stock and reduce the heat to medium-low. Poach the fish until just a touch of translucence remains in the center, 3 to 7 minutes, depending on the thickness of the fish. Lift out the fish with a slotted spoon and let cool on a plate.

Return the pan to high heat and bring the liquid to a boil. Add the asparagus, reduce the heat to medium-low, and simmer until the asparagus is just tender and still bright green, 3 to 5 minutes. Take the pan from the heat and let cool slightly, then purée the soup in batches in a food processor or blender until very smooth. Return the soup to the pan and finely flake the salmon into the soup. Stir in the half-and-half and season to taste with salt and pepper. Reheat the soup over medium-low heat.

To serve, ladle the soup into shallow soup bowls, distributing the salmon evenly.

Makes 4 to 6 servings

Putting the Freeze on Salmon

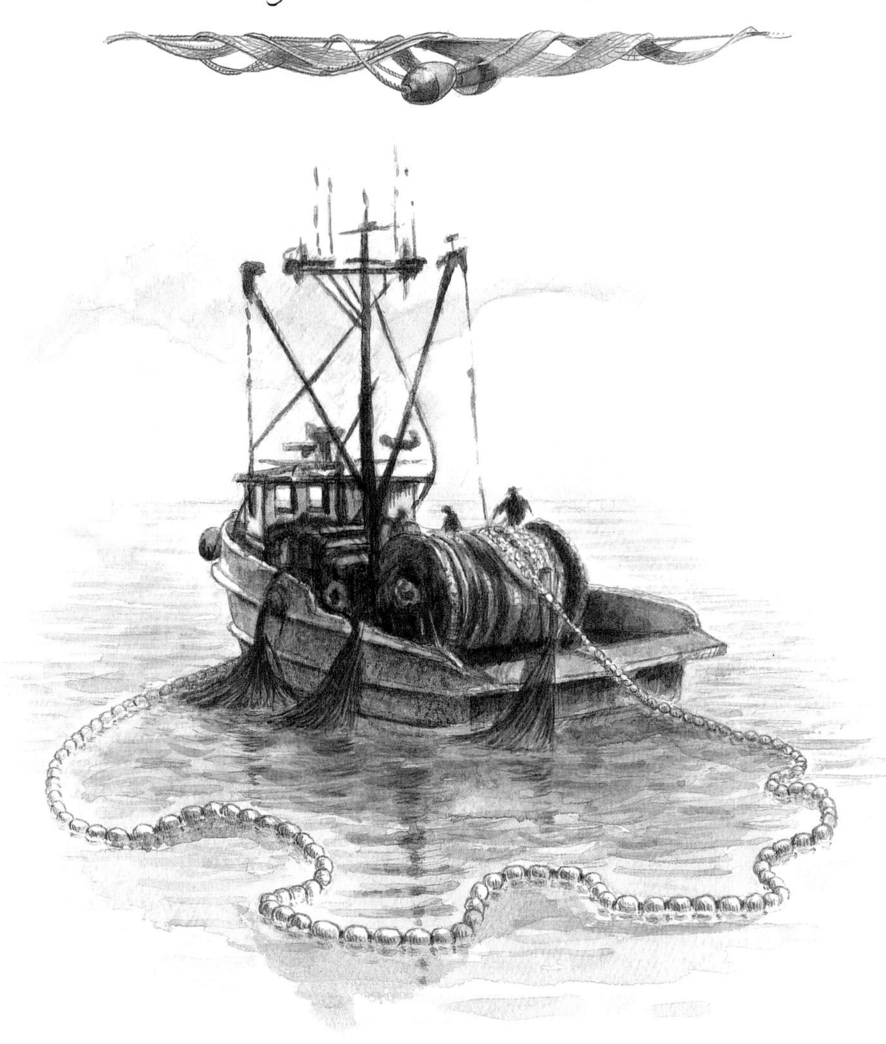

Fresh can be something of a nebulous adjective when it comes to fish. The word is generally understood to mean one of two things, "never frozen" or "of a peak quality." While nothing quite compares to eating a salmon that was recently caught, I'd otherwise encourage you to not get too hung up on the never-frozen element of "fresh" salmon. Often the best piece of fish available to you will have been previously frozen.

Given the vast expanse of waters over which salmon are harvested (particularly in Alaska), it's simply not practical for all those fish to go from fisherman to processor to airport to market quickly enough to still be at their best in an unfrozen state. Much of even the best salmon caught is flash-frozen within hours, sometimes even less than an hour, of being caught. This not only eliminates the imperative of that quick trip to stores and restaurants, but holds the fish in a suspended state—a sort of cryogenic "pause" button—until ready to be consumed, whether a week or a few months later. These account for some of the wild troll-caught salmon that we see in stores and on restaurant menus when there is little or no commercial fishing going on.

The most important factors in the quality of frozen fish are how it is frozen and how it is thawed. The quick answer is, respectively, very fast and very slow. The freezers used by fishermen and processors typically hover well below zero and freeze a whole fish in a matter of a few hours. At those low temperatures, the water in the flesh creates very small crystals of ice that ultimately have a nominal impact on the quality of the flesh of the fish.

Thawing, on the other hand, should be done slowly, ideally overnight in the refrigerator rather than at room temperature, so that those crystals recede gently and the natural moisture of the fish stays imbedded in the flesh rather than seeping out.

Poor freezing at moderately low temperatures creates large crystals of ice as the temperature drops. Those crystals act like micro-blades, puncturing the cell walls in the salmon flesh and compromising its overall texture and moistness. It can have an effect on the way the fish cooks: for example, it may give off excess liquid during cooking, as the broken cell walls can't hold in the moisture they usually would; the fish may also cook more quickly, because the flesh structure is a bit looser after the thaw.

Salmon Pot au Feu

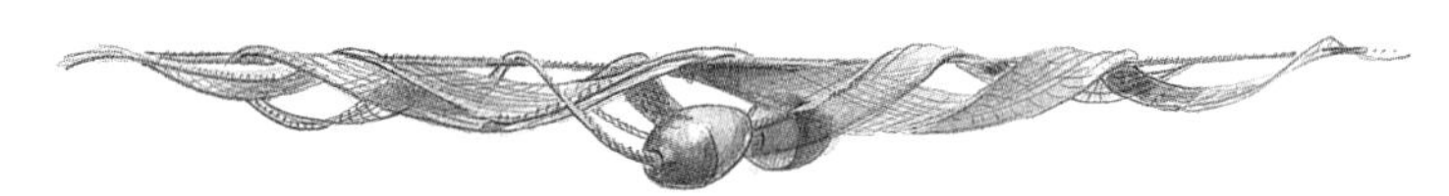

Pot au feu is a classic and simple French recipe of, typically, beef gently simmered with vegetables in a flavorful broth. Translated to a Northwest palette, salmon stars in the recipe, with tender potato, onion, and artichoke accompanying the fish in this tribute to simple, unadulterated flavors. If you're unable to find baby artichokes, you could either use 2 large artichokes, their trimmed bottoms cut into eighths, or use top-quality canned artichoke bottoms, rinsed and cut into eighths. Fingerling potatoes are small thin-skinned potatoes that have a long, slender shape, reminiscent of a pudgy finger.

To save time, you could replace the homemade salmon stock with top-quality purchased fish stock, though you may not need to reduce it depending on how pronounced its flavor is (in which case, use just 4 cups).

¾ pound fingerling potatoes, scrubbed
6 cipollini onions or
  12 small boiling onions, peeled
1 small lemon, halved
6 baby artichokes
4 tarragon sprigs
6 cups salmon stock (see facing page)
Salt and freshly ground white
  or black pepper
1½ pounds salmon fillet,
  skin and pin bones removed

Put the potatoes in a pan of cold salted water and bring to a low boil over medium-high heat. Reduce the heat to medium and simmer until the potatoes are just tender when pierced with the tip of a knife, 12 to 15 minutes, depending on their size. Scoop out the potatoes with a slotted spoon into a bowl and set aside. Return the pan to high heat and bring to a boil. Add the onions to the boiling water, reduce the heat to medium, and simmer until the onions are just barely tender, 8 to 10 minutes. Scoop out the onions with a slotted spoon, add them to the bowl with the potatoes, and set aside, discarding the water.

Squeeze the lemon juice into a medium saucepan of cold water and drop the lemon halves in as well. Use your fingers to trim a couple of outer layers of leaves from the baby artichokes until you reach the tender, paler green leaves toward the center. Trim the stem to about 1 inch and peel away the tough outer green skin from the base and stem. Cut the top down to about 1 inch from the base of the artichoke. Quarter each artichoke, scraping out the choke (some very young artichokes may not have much choke at all), and put the pieces in the saucepan. Bring the water to a boil over medium-high heat, then reduce the heat to medium and simmer until just barely tender, 12 to 15 minutes. Drain well and set aside.

Pluck the tender tops from the tarragon sprigs and set aside for garnish. Mince enough of the remaining tarragon to make about 2 teaspoons and put it in a large saucepan with the salmon stock. Bring the stock to a boil and boil until reduced by about one-third, 12 to 15 minutes. Season the stock with salt and pepper. Quarter the cipollini onions, if using, and cut the potatoes into 1-inch pieces.

Cut the salmon fillet into 1-inch cubes and add the salmon to the stock. Add the artichoke pieces, onions, and potato pieces, cover the pan, and simmer over medium-low heat until just a touch of translucence remains in the center of the salmon cubes, 3 to 5 minutes.

To serve, use a slotted spoon to evenly distributed the salmon and vegetables among 4 shallow soup bowls. Taste the broth for seasoning, adding more salt or pepper to taste, then ladle it into the bowls. Float the reserved tarragon on top and serve right away.

Makes 4 servings

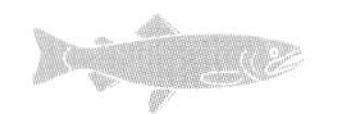

Salmon Stock

Salmon bones are typically not the best choice for fish stock, because the more pronounced flavor might overwhelm the recipe in which the stock is used. But when that recipe has salmon as a centerpiece, it's an ideal time to make salmon stock. You may need to call ahead to your favorite fishmonger to check on the availability of salmon bones. Or, if you buy a whole salmon and fillet it yourself, you may keep the bones for using in stock (if not right away, the bones can be frozen for a month or two before making the stock).

Extra stock can be frozen to use in other recipes. I freeze some stock in premeasured quart quantities. The rest I freeze in ice cube trays and later put the cubes in a heavy-duty, resealable plastic bag. That way, I'm able to use just the amount needed for a recipe (check the volume of 1 cube section in your tray; my trays make cubes of about 2 tablespoons each).

2 pounds salmon bones, rinsed
1 onion, quartered
2 stalks celery, coarsely chopped
1 carrot, sliced
Bouquet garni of parsley, bay leaf (preferably fresh), celery leaves, and tarragon sprigs tied together with kitchen string
1 teaspoon white or black peppercorns

Cut the salmon bones into manageable pieces and put them in a medium stockpot with the onion, celery, carrot, bouquet garni, and peppercorns. Cover the vegetables and bones with cold water (about 2½ quarts) and bring to a low boil over medium-high heat.

Immediately decrease the heat to medium-low and simmer for 40 to 45 minutes, skimming the surface as needed to remove any scum that gathers. (Avoid overcooking the stock or it may pick up bitter elements from the bones.)

Take the pot from the heat and let the stock cool completely. When the stock is cool, slowly pour it through a sieve lined with dampened cheesecloth into a large bowl, leaving behind as much of the solids as possible in the stockpot. If desired, the stock can be reduced after straining to intensify the flavors before using or storing.

Makes about 2 quarts

Grilled Salmon Salad Niçoise

In traditional Niçoise fashion, this substantial salad is composed of a number of ingredients of contrasting colors and textures, salmon replacing the customary tuna. Some of the ingredients may be prepared up to a day ahead—the hard-cooked eggs, potatoes, green beans—to save time just before serving. Allow the vegetables to come to room temperature before serving.

You may re-create this recipe indoors, too. Simply bake the salmon pieces in a hot oven, about 450°F, for 5 to 10 minutes, depending on their thickness. The anchovies are pretty subtle in the dressing; feel free to add another fillet or two to suit your taste.

- 3 eggs
- 1 pound salmon fillet, skin and pin bones removed
- ½ cup extra virgin olive oil
- 3 cloves garlic, finely minced
- Salt and freshly ground white or black pepper
- ¾ pound fingerling potatoes, scrubbed
- 8 ounces green beans, preferably thin young beans, trimmed
- 1 anchovy fillet
- 3 tablespoons white wine vinegar
- 1 tablespoon minced flat-leaf (Italian) parsley
- 2 medium vine-ripe tomatoes, cored and cut into eighths
- ½ cup Niçoise olives or other top-quality dark brined olive

Put the eggs in a medium saucepan with enough cold water to cover them by about 1 inch. Put the pan over high heat and bring to a boil, then reduce the heat to medium-high and set the timer for 10 minutes. Drain the eggs and run cold water over them for a few minutes to stop the cooking and help cool the eggs quickly (which also helps make them easier to peel). Refrigerate until ready to use.

Preheat an outdoor grill.

Cut the salmon fillet into quarters, in roughly squarish pieces. Put 2 tablespoons of the olive oil in a shallow dish and add about half of the garlic with a good pinch each of salt and pepper. Add the salmon pieces and turn to evenly coat the fish in the oil and seasonings; set aside while preparing the other ingredients.

Put the potatoes in a medium pan of cold salted water and bring to a low boil over medium-high heat. Reduce the heat to medium and simmer until the potatoes are just tender when pierced with the tip of a knife, 12 to 15 minutes.

While the potatoes are cooking, bring a medium pan of salted water to a boil and prepare a medium bowl of ice water. Add the green beans to the boiling water and cook until just barely tender and vivid green, 1 to 3 minutes, depending on their size. Drain well and immediately plunge the beans into the ice water to quickly cool and set their color. Drain well and lay out to dry on paper towels. When the potatoes are tender, drain them well and set aside to cool, then cut the potatoes across into ½-inch slices. Peel the hard-cooked eggs and cut them into quarters.

When the grill is hot, lightly rub the grill grate with oil. Lift the salmon pieces from the marinade, allowing excess to drip off, and grill over the hot fire until just a touch of translucence remains in the center of the thickest part, 3 to 5 minutes, turning the pieces once. Transfer to a plate and let cool slightly before serving.

Combine the anchovy fillet with the remaining minced garlic in the bottom of a small bowl and crush with the tines of a fork. Add the vinegar and stir to blend, then add the remaining olive oil in a thin stream, blending constantly with the fork. Stir in the parsley with salt and pepper to taste.

To serve, put the grilled salmon in the center of individual plates and arrange the green beans, potato slices, tomato wedges, and olives around the salmon. Traditionally each ingredient is arranged in its own cluster, but you may distribute them mixed around the salmon if you prefer. Stir the vinaigrette dressing to remix and drizzle it over the vegetables. Serve right away.

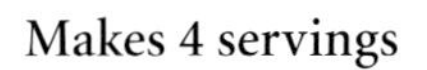

Makes 4 servings

Salmon Salad-Stuffed Tomatoes

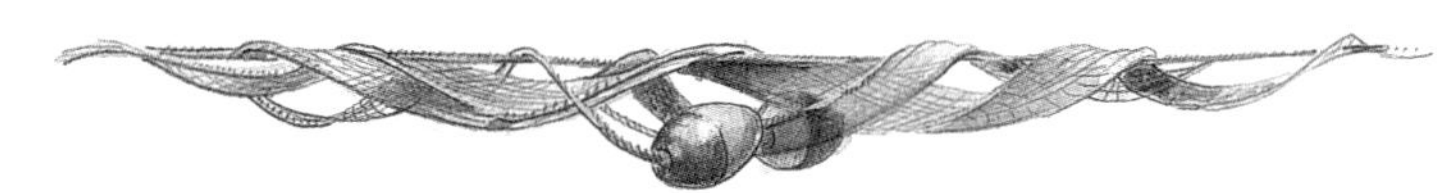

A couple of years ago a friend of mine moved to a beautiful home in the neighborhood of a swish lakeside tennis club. When we started talking about getting together for lunch and a first visit of the new place, I had this incredibly clear image of us sitting on the patio, ostensibly having just played a match of doubles, and sipping iced tea while nibbling on tuna-salad–stuffed tomatoes. I have no idea where that image came from, perhaps some idealized fantasy of being a lady of leisure that somehow equates with that 1950s lunchtime scenario. In honor of the fantasy, I created this retro-style salad, using salmon salad to stuff plump, red tomatoes.

4 medium vine-ripe tomatoes (about 8 ounces each)
Salt and freshly ground white or black pepper
1 pound cooked salmon, finely flaked, skin and pin bones removed (about 2 cups)
¾ cup top-quality mayonnaise, preferably homemade (see box), more to taste
½ cup finely diced peeled cucumber
¼ cup finely diced celery
1 tablespoon plus 1 teaspoon freshly squeezed lemon juice
1 teaspoon minced dill

From each of the tomatoes, cut away the core and trim away the top ½ inch or so. Use a small spoon (a serrated grapefruit spoon, if you have one) to scoop out the tomato flesh and seeds into a small bowl, leaving the inside of the tomato shell relatively even. Add a couple pinches of salt to each tomato shell and use your fingers to rub it around a bit inside the tomato. Line a plate with multiple layers of paper towels and turn the tomatoes upside down on the paper towels to drain. This can be done a few hours in advance; refrigerate the tomatoes until ready to serve.

Retrieve the tomato flesh from the bowl, discarding the watery seeds. Finely chop the tomato flesh and put it in a medium bowl. Add the salmon, ½ cup of the mayonnaise, the cucumber, celery, 1 tablespoon of the lemon juice, ½ teaspoon of the dill, and a good pinch each of salt and pepper. Use a fork to blend the ingredients thoroughly, adding a bit more salt, pepper, or mayonnaise to your taste. Spoon the salmon salad into the tomato shells, pressing down gently as you go to avoid unfilled pockets.

In a small dish, combine the remaining ¼ cup mayonnaise with the remaining 1 teaspoon lemon juice and remaining ½ teaspoon dill. Stir to evenly blend.

To serve, set the stuffed tomatoes on individual plates, top each with a dollop of the dilled mayonnaise, and serve right away.

Makes 4 servings

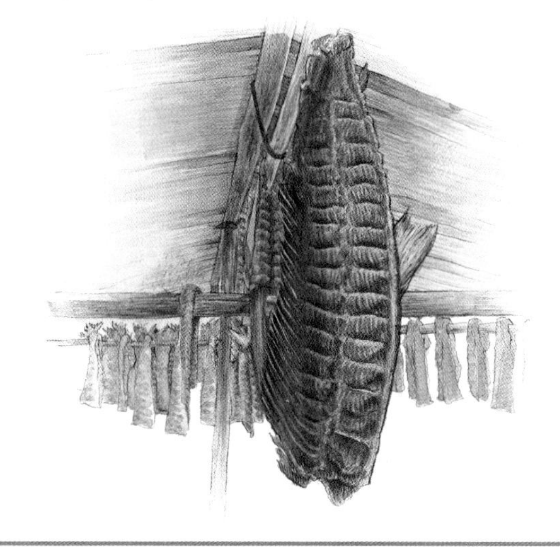

Homemade Mayonnaise

1 egg yolk
2 teaspoons white wine vinegar
¾ cup olive oil (not extra virgin)
Salt and freshly ground white pepper

In a medium bowl, combine the egg yolk with the vinegar and whisk to blend. Begin adding the olive oil a few drops at a time, whisking constantly, until the yolk begins to turn pale and thicken slightly, showing that an emulsion has begun to form. Continue adding the rest of the oil in a thin, steady stream, whisking constantly. Season to taste with salt and pepper.

Alternatively, combine the egg yolk and vinegar in a food processor and pulse to blend. With the blades running, begin adding the oil a few drops at a time until the emulsion begins to form, then continue adding the rest of the oil in a thin, steady stream. Add the salt and pepper to taste and pulse to blend.

Refrigerate the mayonnaise, covered, until ready to serve; it may be made a day or two in advance.

Makes a generous ¾ cup

Tea-Smoked Salmon on Romaine-Almond Salad

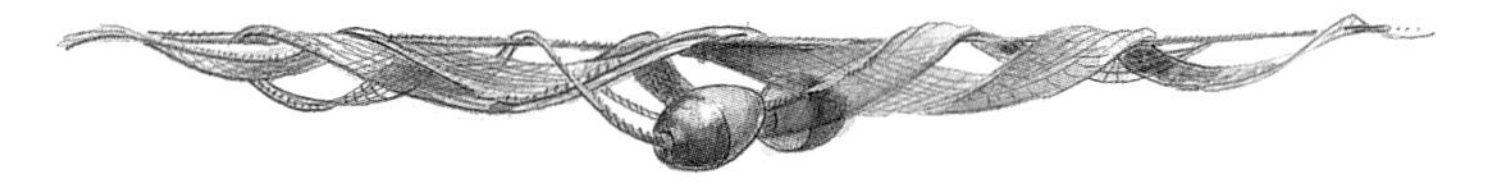

Outstanding resources are available to the food-lover in Seattle, from the Pike Place Market (which celebrates its centennial in 2007) to outstanding chocolatiers and world-class winemakers. One of my favorite shopping destinations is World Merchants [www.worldspice.com], a spice- and tea-lovers nirvana. Owner Tony Hill travels the globe for his trade, witnessing pepper harvest in Hungary, tramping through tea plantations in China, and checking out clove and vanilla groves of Madagascar.

I caught up with Tony shortly after a long tea escapade in China, where he'd seen a man at a roadside stand (2 tables, 5 chairs) tea-smoking duck. I already planned to include tea-smoking in this book, but Tony's description of what he saw the man doing helped inspire this particular technique. After a fascinating tea tasting at his Seattle shop, Tony sent me home with a few ounces of Ruo Kuai tea, a heavy oolong style from the Fujian province of China, with this recipe in mind. This recipe will be particularly delicious with rich salmon, the fat of which will more fully absorb the flavor and aroma of the tea. For a shortcut, you could omit the tea-smoking portion of the recipe and bake the seasoned fillet pieces instead, which will still make for a delicious salad.

2 teaspoons coarse kosher or sea salt
½ teaspoon finely grated orange zest
¼ teaspoon 5-spice powder
⅛ teaspoon freshly ground white or black pepper
4 salmon fillet pieces (about 4 ounces each), skin and pin bones removed
¼ ounce (about ¼ cup) heavy oolong tea such as Ruo Kuai
½ cup water
½ cup freshly squeezed orange juice
1 tablespoon brown sugar
2 tablespoons rice wine vinegar or white wine vinegar
2 teaspoons sesame oil
½ teaspoon soy sauce
1 small head romaine, rinsed, dried, and cut into ½-inch strips
1 medium carrot, cut into julienne strips or coarsely grated
¼ cup sliced almonds, toasted

Combine the salt, orange zest, 5-spice powder, and pepper in a small bowl and rub the seasonings between your fingers for a minute or two to extract some of the essential oils from the orange zest to coat the salt. Sprinkle the seasoning mix evenly over the salmon fillet pieces and arrange them on a round wire rack that will fit snugly inside your wok.

Put the tea in a medium bowl. Bring the water just to a boil, set aside for a minute or two to cool just a bit, and pour the hot water over the tea. Set aside to steep for about

4 minutes, then strain, reserving both the liquid and the leaves. Pat the leaves dry with paper towels to remove excess water.

Line a wok with 2 overlapping pieces of foil so that the ends and sides overhang by 2 to 3 inches most of the way around. Put the tea leaves in the bottom of the wok and spread them out a bit so they're in a thin layer rather than a pile. Set the wok over high heat until the tea begins to gently smoke, 1 to 2 minutes.

Carefully set the rack with the salmon in the wok and cover with the lid (it's okay to turn off the heat under the wok while doing this), crimping down the foil around the lip of the lid to provide a good seal. I use kitchen tongs to do this, to avoid burning myself. Turn the heat to medium-high and cook for 5 minutes. Turn the heat off and let the wok sit undisturbed for 15 minutes or so.

While the salmon is resting, combine the orange juice, ¼ cup of the steeped tea, and the brown sugar in a small saucepan and bring just to a boil over medium-high heat. Transfer 3 tablespoons of the mixture to a medium bowl and set aside for the salad. Boil the remaining juice mixture over medium heat until reduced by about three-quarters, to a slightly thickened glaze, 5 to 7 minutes. Set aside.

Remove the lid from the wok and lightly brush the salmon pieces with the orange-tea glaze. Whisk the rice wine vinegar, sesame oil, and soy sauce into the reserved orange juice mixture and season to taste with salt and pepper. Add the romaine, carrot, and sliced almonds. Toss to mix well.

To serve, arrange the salad on individual plates, top the salad with the tea-smoked salmon, and serve right away.

Makes 4 servings

Green Lentil Salad with Salmon and Mustard Cream

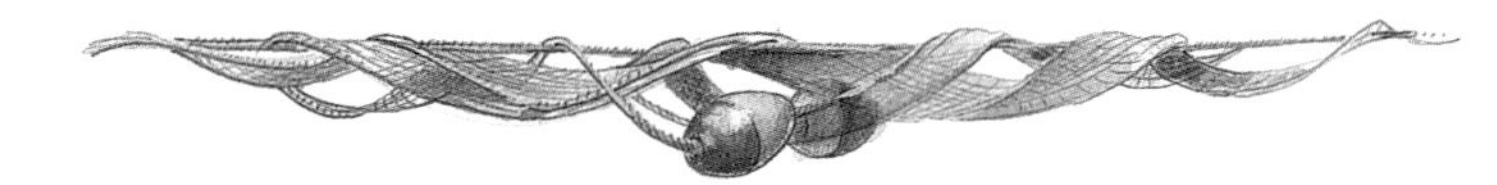

Raise your hand if you know that Washington state produced more lentils than any other of the United States. It is mighty surprising the number of foods for which the Northwest is a top producer. With Idaho close behind, the two states produce nearly all the lentils grown in the country.

I particularly love small, green lentils for this recipe. They have a wonderful, distinct nutty flavor and hold their shape well through cooking. This type is commonly known as *du Puy* lentils in France, though the lentil is grown in the Northwest as well. Regular brown lentils may be used, but take care to not overcook them or they will begin to fall apart.

1½ cups green lentils
1 thick slice onion pierced with 2 whole cloves
1 bay leaf
4 teaspoons thyme leaves
1 clove garlic, minced
3 cups water, more if needed
3 tablespoons red wine vinegar
1 tablespoon minced shallot or onion
1 tablespoon plus 2 teaspoons Dijon mustard
Salt and freshly ground white or black pepper
⅓ cup plus 1 tablespoon olive oil
1 pound salmon fillet, skin and pin bones removed, cut into ½-inch cubes
⅓ cup heavy cream

Pick over the lentils to remove any stones or other debris. Put the lentils in a medium saucepan with the onion slice, bay leaf, 2 teaspoons of the thyme leaves, the garlic, and water. Bring just to a boil over medium-high heat, then lower the heat to medium-low and simmer, uncovered, until the lentils are tender, 20 to 30 minutes, adding more hot water if needed so the lentils remain just covered.

Meanwhile, combine the vinegar, shallot, 2 teaspoons of the mustard, and the remaining 2 teaspoons of the thyme leaves in a large bowl with a good pinch of salt. Whisk to mix and set aside for a few minutes to allow the salt to dissolve. Whisk in ⅓ cup of the olive oil, then season the dressing to taste with pepper.

When the lentils are cooked, drain them well, discarding the onion and bay leaf. Add the warm lentils to the vinaigrette and stir gently to evenly mix without breaking up the lentils. Taste the lentils for seasoning and set aside, covered.

Preheat the broiler. Line a baking sheet with foil.

Put the cubed salmon in a medium bowl and drizzle the remaining 1 tablespoon olive oil over. Season with a pinch each of salt and pepper and toss gently to evenly coat the salmon cubes. Put the salmon cubes on the baking sheet, spreading them out for even cooking. Broil the salmon about 4 inches from the heat until just a touch of translucence remains in the center of the thickest part, 3 to 5 minutes. While the salmon is cooking, whip the cream to form medium peaks, then whisk in the remaining 1 tablespoon of the mustard.

To serve, add the salmon cubes to the lentil salad and toss gently to mix. Spoon the salad on individual plates, top with a dollop of the mustard cream, and serve right away.

Makes 4 servings

Salmon Burgers with Basil Mayonnaise

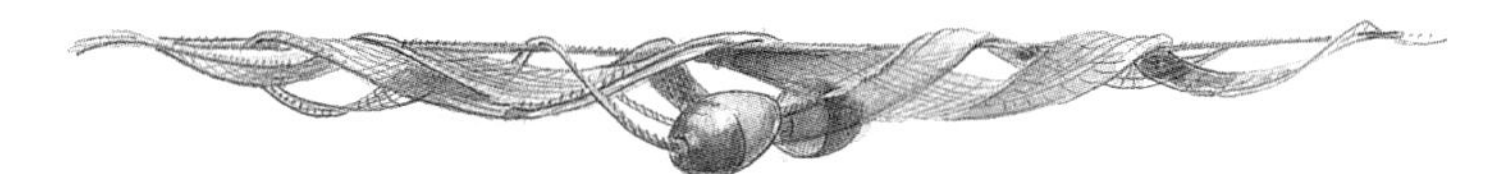

It's hardly summer without a grilled burger now and then, and even lovely salmon can get in on the fun. Basil oil is a heady infusion of fresh basil leaves into good-quality oil. It is available in well-stocked grocery stores and specialty food shops, but is optional for this recipe. If not using the basil oil, consider adding another tablespoon or two of freshly minced basil. You may omit the homemade mayonnaise if you prefer, simply stirring basil into top-quality prepared mayonnaise.

1½ pounds salmon fillet, skin and pin bones removed
½ cup minced red onion
2 tablespoons minced basil
1 teaspoon finely grated lemon zest
1 teaspoon salt
¼ teaspoon freshly ground white or black pepper
4 Kaiser rolls or hamburger buns
4 crisp lettuce leaves
4 large tomato slices

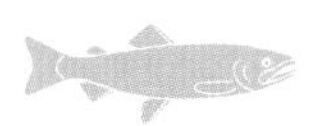

Basil Mayonnaise

1 egg yolk
1 tablespoon white wine vinegar
¾ cup olive oil (not extra virgin)
2 tablespoons minced basil
2 to 3 tablespoons basil oil (optional)
Salt and freshly ground white or black pepper

For the basil mayonnaise, combine the egg yolk and vinegar in a medium bowl and whisk to blend. Begin adding the olive oil a drop at a time, whisking constantly, until the yolk begins to turn pale and thicken slightly, showing that an emulsion has begun to form. Continue adding the rest of the oil in a thin, steady stream, whisking constantly, then whisk in the basil and basil oil, if using, with salt and pepper to taste. (Alternatively, combine the egg yolk and vinegar in a food processor and pulse to blend. With the blades running, begin adding the oil a few drops at a time, then continue adding the rest in a thin, steady stream. Add the basil and basil oil with salt and pepper to taste and pulse to blend.) Refrigerate the mayonnaise until ready to serve; it will have a fuller, more balanced flavor if made at least 1 hour before serving and can be made 1 to 2 days in advance.

Preheat an outdoor grill.

Cut the salmon fillet into medium dice and pulse it a few times in a food processor to finely chop without making a purée. Alternatively, pass the salmon pieces through the medium plate of a meat grinder. Put the salmon in a large bowl with the onion, basil, lemon zest, salt, and pepper. Stir to evenly mix, then form the salmon mixture into 4 burgers, about 4 inches across and 1 inch thick.

When the grill is heated, lightly rub the grill grate with oil and grill the burgers until they are just opaque through and moderately browned, 3 to 4 minutes per side. While the burgers are cooking, toast the buns on the outer edge of the grill, if you like.

To serve, set the salmon burgers on the bottom bun, top with a good dollop of the basil mayonnaise, followed by the lettuce, tomato, and the top bun. Serve right away.

Makes 4 servings

Salmon BLT

While the classic BLT is pretty close to sandwich perfection as far as I'm concerned, the combination gets even better with the addition of freshly sautéed salmon. The trick is to not skimp on any of the ingredients: thick-cut bacon, generous slices of tomato, and a good, crisp mound of lettuce. This recipe is at its best during the late summer when Northwest tomatoes are at their juicy peak of ripeness.

You should start with one whole fillet piece for this recipe, preferably the thinner tail end, which will be easiest to cut into thin escalope pieces. If you have only thicker pieces, cut away the skin and cut the salmon into ¾-inch slices, using 2 to 3 slices per sandwich.

8 thick strips top-quality bacon, preferably wood smoked
8 slices white or whole-wheat bread, lightly toasted
4 to 6 large leaves crisp lettuce, rinsed and patted dry
1 large or 2 small heirloom tomatoes, cored and sliced
¾ pound salmon fillet, pin bones removed
2 tablespoons olive oil
Salt and freshly ground white or black pepper
¼ cup top-quality mayonnaise, preferably homemade (page 41), more to taste

Preheat the oven to 400°F. Lay the bacon strips on a rimmed baking sheet and bake until the bacon is crisp, about 15 minutes, turning the strips once or twice so they cook evenly. Transfer the bacon to paper towels to drain.

Lay 4 of the toast pieces on the work surface and top each with the lettuce, followed by the tomato slices (overlapping, if needed), and bacon, breaking it into pieces as needed to evenly cover the tomatoes.

Beginning about 4 or 5 inches in from the thinner end of the salmon fillet piece, use a large, sharp knife to cut an escalope slice about ¼ inch thick: with the knife at about a 45-degree angle, cut toward the tail end, cutting the flesh from the skin where the two meet. Repeat to make 3 more escalopes, beginning each about 1 inch in from the previous slice. (You will have a bit of salmon left, which can be saved for another use, or thinly sliced to add to the sandwiches as well.)

Heat the oil in a large skillet over medium heat. Season the salmon pieces on both sides with salt and pepper, then add them to the skillet and cook until the salmon has just a touch of translucence in the center, about 1 minute per side.

Set the salmon on top of the bacon. Spread the mayonnaise on the remaining slices of toast and top off the sandwiches. Cut across into triangles and serve right away.

Makes 4 servings

Salmon Soft Tacos with Lime Crème Fraîche

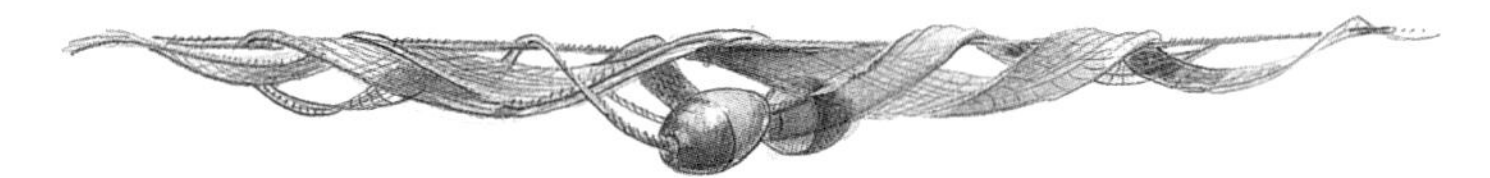

Classic fish tacos, like those served in and around San Diego, are often made with batter-fried strips of fish. While I have nothing against fried fish, I prefer this simple, cleanly flavored baked version for these salmon tacos. Marinating the salmon in some of the salsa verde is an optional step to add a touch more flavor. The dish would also be tasty with grilled salmon rather than baked.

- 1 pound salmon fillet, skin and pin bones removed
- 1 cup salsa verde
- ½ cup crème fraîche or sour cream
- 3 tablespoons freshly squeezed lime juice
- 2 teaspoons finely grated lime zest
- Salt and freshly ground white or black pepper
- 12 small white corn tortillas
- ¼ head green cabbage, cored and finely shredded
- 1 medium tomato, cored and finely chopped

Cut the salmon fillet crosswise into strips about 1 inch thick and set them in a shallow dish. Pour half of the salsa verde over and turn the salmon pieces to evenly coat them. Set aside for 30 minutes (or up to 4 hours, refrigerated).

Preheat the oven to 350°F. Line a baking sheet with foil and lightly oil the foil.

In a small bowl, stir together the crème fraîche, lime juice, lime zest, and a pinch of salt; set aside. Wrap the corn tortillas in foil and heat them in the oven for about 5 minutes.

Meanwhile, lift the salmon pieces from the salsa, allowing excess to drip off, and arrange them on the prepared baking sheet; discard the marinade. Bake until the salmon is just opaque through, 8 to 10 minutes.

To serve, set a warm tortilla on each individual plate and top with a piece or two of the baked salmon. Add a spoonful of the remaining salsa verde, some of the shredded cabbage, and a spoonful or two of the tomato. Drizzle some of the lime crème fraîche over and fold the taco in half. Continue making the remaining tacos alongside the first on each plate. Serve right away.

Makes 4 to 6 servings

Appetizers

Ginger and Star Anise Hot-Smoked Salmon

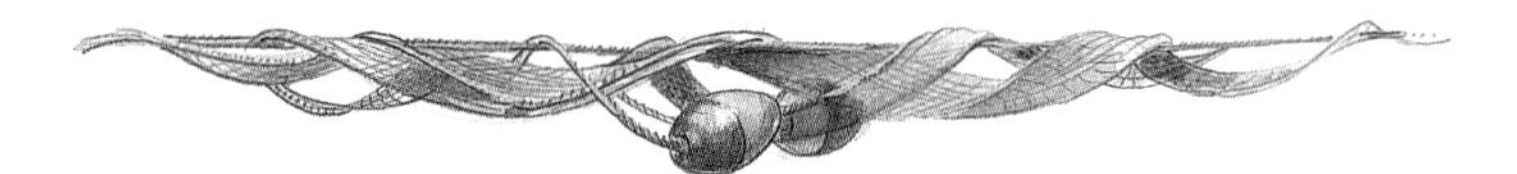

Despite the fact that smoked salmon of all types is available in stores today, nothing beats salmon that you have smoked yourself at home. Not only will it be fresher, but you'll be able to make minor tweaks in the recipe to suit your taste and style preferences. Consider using other spices, such as black pepper or crushed coriander seed, maybe maple syrup in place of the brown sugar, or add strips of orange zest to the brine. Smoked salmon is versatile, a wonderful snack for a picnic or appetizer, a tasty addition to pasta, or for topping cream-cheese-spread bagels (page 28).

Most any outdoor covered grill may be used for smoking, though it's important to set up indirect heat so that the fish cooks more slowly and gently than with traditional grilling. My classic kettle-style Weber doubles as a good smoker, though I also use an actual smoker as well, which is taller in proportion and has more room for fish and better control over heat. I offer instructions here for a standard grill, but if you have a smoker by all means use it, following the manufacturer's instructions. Smoking time will vary with the thickness of the fish you use, the type of smoker, level of heat, outdoor temperatures, and other variables, so keep your eye on things and judge more by the fish than by the timer. Smoking is definitely more art than science.

5 cups warm water, more if needed
2 cups packed light brown sugar
1 cup kosher salt
8 star anise, lightly crushed
12 slices (¼ inch thick) ginger, cut in julienne strips
1 salmon fillet piece (about 2 pounds), skin on, pin bones removed
2 cups wood smoking chips (such as alder, apple, or hickory)

Make a brine by combining the water, brown sugar, salt, star anise, and ginger in a large shallow dish such as a 9-by-13-inch baking dish. Stir occasionally until the sugar and salt are fully dissolved; set aside until the water cools to room temperature.

When the brine has cooled, add the salmon skin-side up. The salmon should be fully submerged; add a bit more cool water if needed. Cover the dish with plastic wrap and refrigerate for at least 4 and up to 10 hours. (Avoid brining the fish too long or it will take on a too-salty flavor.) Take the fish from the brine, rinse lightly under cold water, and dry well with paper towels. Set the salmon fillet, skin-side down, on a wire rack and air dry on the counter until the surface is no longer sticky, about 1 hour. This step helps form a pellicle, or thin barrier, on the surface of the flesh to help hold in moisture during smoking. If you have a small fan, set it up to blow gently on the salmon to speed up the drying.

About 30 minutes before ready to smoke, put the wood chips in a bowl and cover with cold water. Set aside to soak.

Preheat a batch of charcoal in your grill (if you have a gas grill, preheat according to manufacturer's instructions for smoking). When the coals are glowing, carefully form 2 mounds of coals on opposite sides of the grill. Put an 8-inch-square (or similar sized) foil pan on the rack between the coals and add a couple cups of water to the pan. Quickly but thoroughly drain the wood chips and scatter them over the charcoal mounds. Put the grill grate on the grill and lightly rub the grill grate with oil. Lay the salmon fillet in the center of the grate and cover with the lid. Smoke until the salmon is just cooked through and the fish has an amber hue from the smoke, about 30 minutes in a traditional grill or up to 1 hour in a smoker.

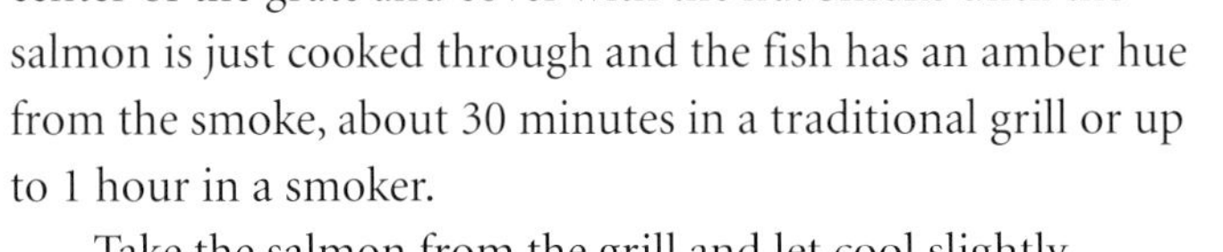

Take the salmon from the grill and let cool slightly, or completely, before serving.

Makes 8 to 12 servings

Salmon and Scallop Terrine with Watercress Sauce

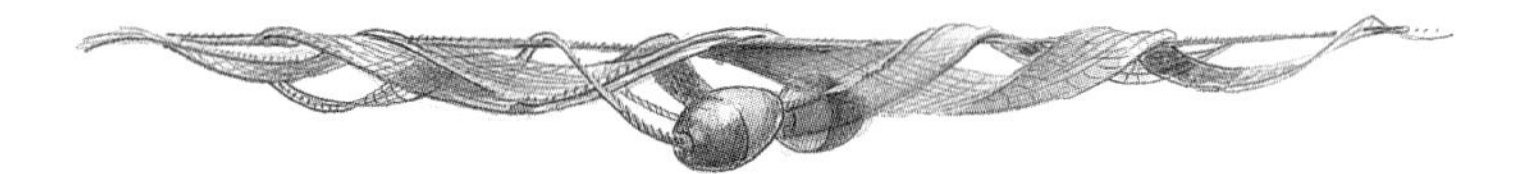

While not a complicated recipe, this dish isn't exactly a quick-fix appetizer. You'll be thrilled with the results, though—colorful layers of salmon and spinach mousse embellished with pieces of scallop, perfect for a formal sit-down dinner party or served on a cocktail buffet. If you don't have a terrine mold, you may also use another mold of the same volume or a loaf pan. The terrine may be served either warm from the oven or chilled. If chilled, consider replacing the watercress sauce with an herbed mayonnaise, cold tomato coulis, or plain yogurt flavored with minced green onions and garlic.

1⅓ pounds salmon fillet, skin and pin bones removed
2 eggs
1¼ cups half-and-half or heavy cream
½ teaspoon salt
2 pinches freshly ground white or black pepper
2 pinches freshly grated or ground nutmeg
1 package (10 ounces) frozen spinach, thawed
¾ pound bay scallops, halved, or sea scallops, cut into quarters or eighths

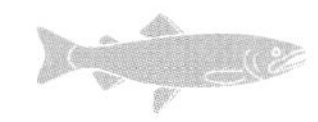

Watercress Sauce

2 tablespoons unsalted butter
1 cup chopped onion
1 cup salmon stock (page 37) or fish stock
¾ cup dry white wine
½ cup heavy cream
1 cup lightly packed watercress leaves (about 2 ounces), plus a few sprigs for garnish

Cut the salmon into large chunks and put it in the bowl of a food processor. Pulse a few times to mince. Add 1 of the eggs, ¾ cup of the half-and-half, ¼ teaspoon of the salt, a pinch of pepper, and a pinch of nutmeg. Process until smooth and light in color, about 1 minute. Transfer to a bowl and set aside.

Clean the processor bowl to make the spinach mousse. Squeeze the spinach to remove as much moisture as possible and put it in the bowl of the food processor. Add the remaining

egg, remaining ½ cup half-and-half, remaining salt, pepper, and nutmeg. Process until very smooth and light in color, 1 to 2 minutes.

Preheat the oven to 350°F. Lightly butter a terrine mold and line it with a large piece of plastic wrap, with excess hanging over each side.

Spoon about half of the salmon mousse mixture into the terrine, smoothing the top. Scatter about half of the scallops over. Spoon the spinach mousse over and smooth the top, pressing down gently. Scatter the remaining scallops over and top with the remaining salmon mousse. Gently rap the terrine on the counter to eliminate air pockets. Fold the plastic wrap ends over the mousse and top with the lid (or securely cover with foil).

Set the terrine in a larger baking dish and fill the dish halfway with hot water. Bake the terrine until the center of the terrine reads 145°F on an instant-read thermometer (otherwise insert a slender metal skewer into the terrine for 20 seconds and touch it carefully against the back of your hand; it should be quite hot to the touch), about 1 hour 15 minutes.

While the terrine is baking, make the sauce. Melt the butter in a medium saucepan over medium heat. Add the onion and cook until tender and aromatic, 3 to 5 minutes. Add the stock and wine and bring to a boil over high heat. Reduce the heat to medium-high and boil until reduced by half. Add the cream and repeat, boiling again to reduce by about half. Finally add the watercress leaves and cook until tender and still vivid green, about 1 minute. Take the pan from the heat and let cool for a few minutes, then purée in a blender until smooth. Return the mixture to the pan, season the sauce to taste with salt and pepper, and keep warm over very low heat. (The sauce is good chilled as well.)

Transfer the terrine to a wire rack and carefully remove the lid. Let the terrine cool for at least 10 minutes, then drain off any liquid and invert the terrine onto a cutting board. Remove the plastic wrap and let sit another few minutes, draining off any accumulated liquid.

To serve, cut the terrine into slices and arrange on individual plates. Spoon the watercress sauce around, garnish with watercress sprigs, and serve right away. The terrine could also be chilled before slicing to serve cold.

Makes 12 to 16 servings

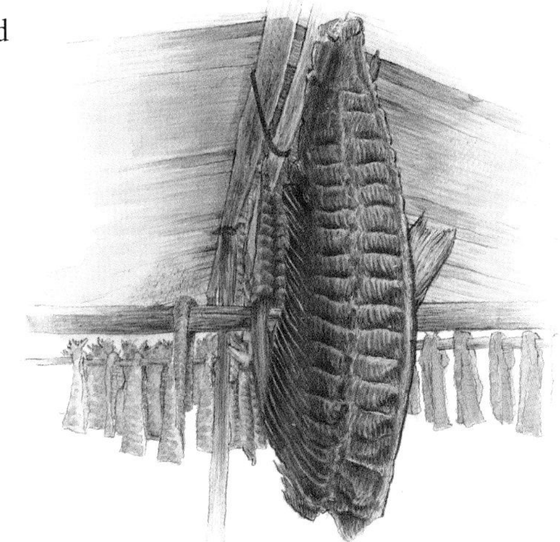

Lomi Lomi Salmon

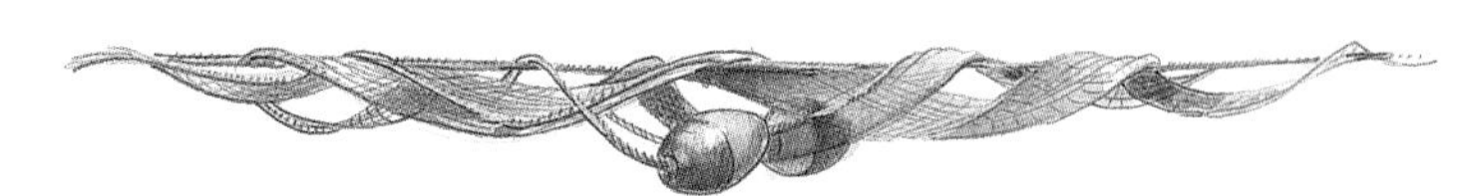

A traditional dish from the Hawaiian luau menu, lomi lomi is classically made with salmon that has been salted for many hours, often overnight, then rinsed and chopped, but this variation uses fresh salmon instead. The use of lime juice will slightly firm up the salmon flesh, as with ceviche, and will add a bright flavor to the salad though it's a misnomer to consider that the juice "cooks" the fish in any way. The salmon here is still raw, which can be harmful for people with compromised immune systems. An option is to use previously frozen salmon, or to lightly poach the fish pieces just until cooked through, then let cool and proceed as directed.

Serving the lomi lomi with taro chips alongside would follow the Pacific Islands inspiration of the recipe, but tortilla chips are a good option as well. You may also serve the lomi lomi spooned into endive leaves or simply on a bed of shredded lettuce as a salad.

¾ pound salmon fillet, skin and pin bones removed
1 large vine-ripe tomato, cored, seeded, and cut into ¼-inch dice
1 cup finely chopped Walla Walla Sweet onion or other sweet onion
¼ cup freshly squeezed lime juice
1 teaspoon hot pepper sauce or finely minced chile pepper (such as serrano or jalapeño), more to taste
Salt
Taro chips or other chips, for serving

Cut the salmon into ¼-inch slices, then across into slivers about ¼ inch thick (traditionally the salmon is shredded, though you could simply dice the salmon instead if you prefer). Put the salmon in a large bowl with the tomato, onion, lime juice, and pepper sauce. Season to taste with salt, toss well to evenly mix, and refrigerate for 30 minutes to 1 hour before serving.

To serve, spoon the lomi lomi salmon onto individual plates or into a single serving bowl, with taro or other chips alongside.

Makes 8 servings

Deviled Salmon Skewers

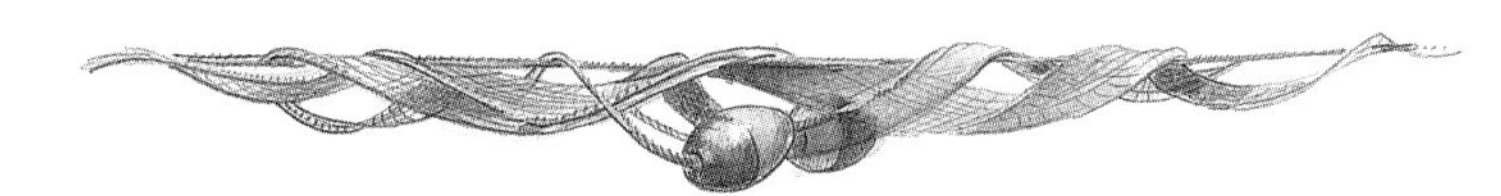

There is some devilish zesty character in this salmon recipe. It makes for great backyard barbecue fare, offering your friends something to nibble on while the main event is hitting the grill. The same recipe could be used for larger salmon steaks or fillet pieces, to grill or broil and serve as a main course instead.

1 pound salmon fillet,
  skin and pin bones removed
¼ cup Worcestershire sauce
2 tablespoons dry vermouth
  or dry white wine
2 tablespoons Dijon mustard
1 teaspoon hot pepper sauce,
  more to taste
6 to 8 green onions, trimmed and cut
  into 1½-inch pieces

Preheat an outdoor grill or the broiler. Soak 12 small (6-inch) bamboo skewers in a bowl of cold water for 30 minutes.

Cut the salmon fillet into 1-inch cubes. Combine the Worcestershire sauce, vermouth, mustard, and hot pepper sauce in a shallow dish and stir to evenly mix. Add the salmon cubes and stir gently so they are evenly coated with the marinade. Set aside for 15 to 30 minutes to marinate.

Drain the skewers and thread 3 marinated salmon cubes onto each skewer, skewering 1 to 2 pieces of green onion between the cubes.

When the grill is hot, lightly rub the grate with oil or lightly oil a foil-lined baking sheet if broiling. Grill or broil the salmon skewers until just a touch of translucence remains in the center, 3 to 5 minutes, turning the skewers once or twice.

Arrange the skewers on individual plates or on a serving platter and serve right away.

Makes 4 to 6 servings

Pot Stickers with Salmon and Shiitake Mushrooms

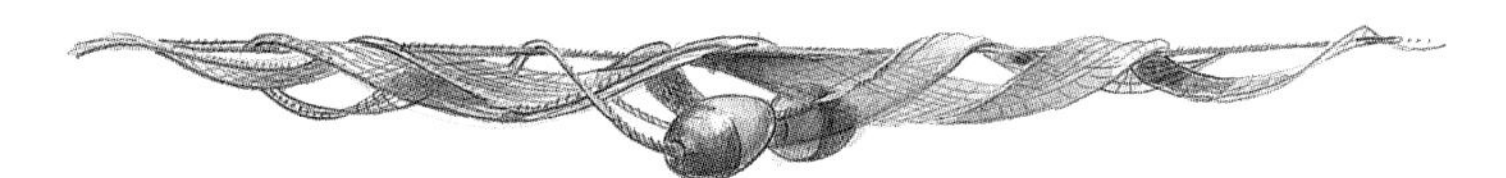

The earthy flavor of shiitake mushrooms plays off rich salmon in these crispy-tender pot stickers, which may be served either as an appetizer or on a large platter for a buffet or cocktail party. The pot stickers may be made up to a few hours in advance and refrigerated, but they will be at their best cooked shortly before serving. In Asian markets, you can find a simple and inexpensive tool to make filling and folding pot stickers easier.

About 24 pot sticker wrappers
4 tablespoons vegetable oil
¾ cup salmon stock (page 37), vegetable stock, or water
Cilantro sprigs, for garnish

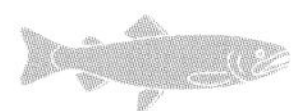

Salmon and Shiitake Filling

1 tablespoon vegetable oil
¼ cup finely chopped onion
6 ounces shiitake mushrooms, stemmed and finely chopped
2 teaspoons minced or grated ginger
2 teaspoons soy sauce
Pinch dried red pepper flakes (optional)
8 ounces salmon fillet, skin and pin bones removed, finely diced
1 tablespoon minced cilantro
½ teaspoon sesame oil

Dipping Sauce

¼ cup soy sauce
¼ cup salmon stock (page 37), vegetable stock, or water
2 tablespoons Chinese rice wine or dry sherry
2 teaspoons sesame oil
¼ teaspoon minced or grated ginger
Pinch dried red pepper flakes

For the salmon and shiitake filling, heat the oil in a medium skillet over medium heat. Add the onion and cook, stirring, until tender and aromatic, 2 to 3 minutes. Add the shiitake mushrooms and cook, stirring often, until the mushrooms are tender and any liquid that they give off has evaporated, about 5 minutes. Add the ginger, soy sauce, and pepper flakes (if using) and cook, stirring, for 1 minute longer.

Take the skillet from the heat and let cool for a few minutes. Add the salmon, cilantro, and sesame oil and stir until evenly blended.

Set a few pot sticker wrappers on the work surface, covering the rest with a kitchen towel to keep them from drying out. Set a small dish of water on the counter nearby. Top each of the pot sticker wrappers with about 2 teaspoons of the filling. Dip your finger in the water and lightly rub some water around the edge of each wrapper. Draw 2 sides of each wrapper up over the filling, pressing the edges together to seal well and pinching little pleats into the dough in 3 or 4 places around the arc of the edge. The shape of the pot sticker should be vertical, with a flat bottom and the sealed edge pointing upwards. Set the filled pot stickers on a lightly floured baking sheet and cover with a kitchen towel while filling the remaining pot stickers.

For the dipping sauce, combine the soy sauce, stock, rice wine, sesame oil, ginger, and pepper flakes in a small bowl and stir to mix. Set aside while cooking the pot stickers.

Heat 2 tablespoons of the oil in each of 2 large skillets (or cook half the pot stickers at a time in 1 skillet) over medium heat and add the pot stickers, so they are touching as little as possible. Cook until the bottoms of the pot stickers begin to brown, 2 to 3 minutes. Drizzle the stock (half, if cooking in batches) around the pot stickers and immediately cover the skillet with its lid or a large piece of foil. Cook until the pot stickers are tender and most of the liquid has evaporated, 4 to 6 minutes. Remove the lid and cook over medium-high heat until any remaining liquid has evaporated and the pot stickers are nicely browned and crisp on the bottom and cooked through, 2 to 3 minutes longer.

To serve, arrange the pot stickers on individual plates. Stir the dipping sauce to mix and pour it into individual small bowls. Set the sauce alongside the pot stickers, garnish with cilantro sprigs, and serve right away.

Makes 4 to 6 servings

Steamed Salmon in Cabbage Packets on Beurre Rouge

Okay, so the sauce isn't exactly *rouge* (red), but this cousin of *beurre blanc* does start with a reduction of red wine rather than the traditional white, thus the name. It makes for an interesting change of pace and works well with the more pronounced flavor of salmon. For a main course serving, you could double the amount of salmon used, forming larger cabbage packets that will need to steam for about 4 minutes longer.

To steam dishes such as this, I use the classic and inexpensive stackable bamboo steamer baskets available in cookware stores and Asian markets.

1 head green cabbage
1 pound salmon fillet, skin and pin bones removed
1 tablespoon olive oil
Salt and freshly ground white or black pepper
2 tablespoons minced shallot
1 tablespoon minced flat-leaf (Italian) parsley, plus more for garnish

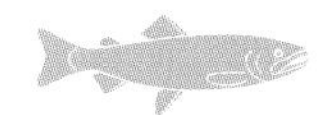

Beurre Rouge

½ cup dry red wine
1 tablespoon red wine vinegar
1 shallot, minced
1 cup unsalted butter, cut into pieces and chilled
1½ teaspoons minced flat-leaf (Italian) parsley

Carefully cut the core from the cabbage and peel away any bruised outer leaves. Peel away 8 other large whole leaves and reserve the rest of the cabbage for another use. Bring a large pan of salted water to a boil and prepare a large bowl of ice water. Add the cabbage leaves to the boiling water and blanch until they are quite tender, 2 to 3 minutes. Use tongs to lift out the leaves by the stem ends and put them immediately in the ice water to quickly cool, which avoids overcooking and sets the color. When fully chilled, drain the leaves well and dry on several layers of paper towel.

Cut the salmon fillet into 6 even pieces. If the fillet piece you have is quite wide, you might want to first cut it in half lengthwise, then across into even pieces. Lay the 6 largest

cabbage leaves, more attractive side down, on the work surface and set a salmon piece in the center of each leaf. Drizzle the olive oil over the fish and rub it all over. Season with salt and pepper and scatter the shallot and parsley over the salmon. Fold the top and bottom edges of the cabbage over the salmon, then fold in both sides to fully enclose the fish (if smaller leaves don't fully enclose the salmon, use an additional piece of the remaining blanched cabbage leaves). Turn the packets over so the ends are underneath and set the packets directly on the steamer rack, or on a lightly oiled heatproof plate that will fit inside your steamer, depending on the kind of steamer you have. Put 2 to 3 inches of water in the wok or bottom of the steamer and bring to a boil, then add the steamer top. Cover and steam until just a touch of translucence remains in the center of the thickest part of the salmon (you can make a small slit in one of the larger packets with a small knife to peek), 12 to 15 minutes.

While the salmon is steaming, make the beurre rouge. Combine the wine, vinegar, and shallot in a small heavy saucepan and bring to a boil over high heat. Reduce the heat to medium-high and continue to boil until there is only about 1 tablespoon of liquid remaining, about 5 minutes. Reduce the heat to low and begin adding the butter in pieces, constantly whisking between each addition so the cold butter melts slowly and creates a creamy sauce. Take the pan off the heat as needed to avoid overheating the sauce, which will cause the butter to "break" and the sauce to become oily. When all the butter has been added, whisk in the parsley with salt and pepper to taste. Keep the sauce warm over very low heat until ready to serve.

To serve, drain the salmon packets on a paper towel to remove excess water and set the packets seam-side down on individual plates. Spoon the beurre rouge around the packets, sprinkle chopped parsley over, and serve right away.

Makes 6 servings

The Fat of Kings (and Other Salmon)

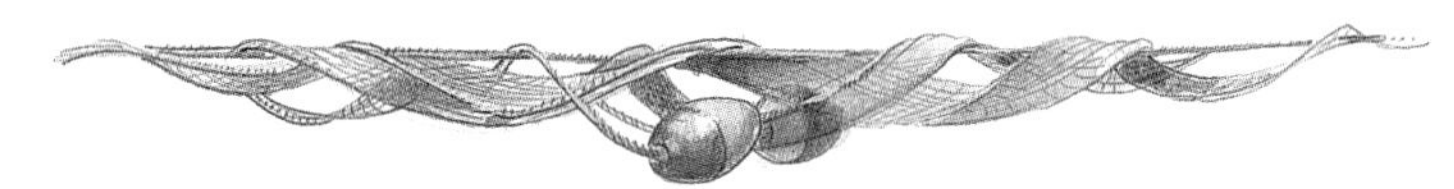

There are pronounced striations—more in some species, less in others—of ivory-to-white fat throughout the flesh of salmon, which is comparable to the marbling of fat in a steak. And this fat has a similar effect on the flesh as it does in steak, keeping it moist and flavorful during cooking, assuring a premium eating experience.

With salmon, the bonus is that this fat not only helps boost the flavor of the fish, but it also carries the beneficial omega-3 essential fatty acids that are understood to be important for our health. The connection originated with study of the Eskimos of Greenland, whose diet relied heavily on food from the sea and who suffered surprisingly little heart disease, rheumatoid arthritis, and psoriasis, among other ailments. Eventually researchers made the omega-3 connection, and appreciation for the fat of salmon and other rich fish has continually grown since that time.

King salmon have the highest fat levels of all the Pacific salmon so they carry the most omega-3 fatty acids in their flesh. In descending order of fat levels are sockeye, pink, coho, and chum. Other key sources include herring, bluefish, and sardines.

Gin- and Juniper-Cured Salmon

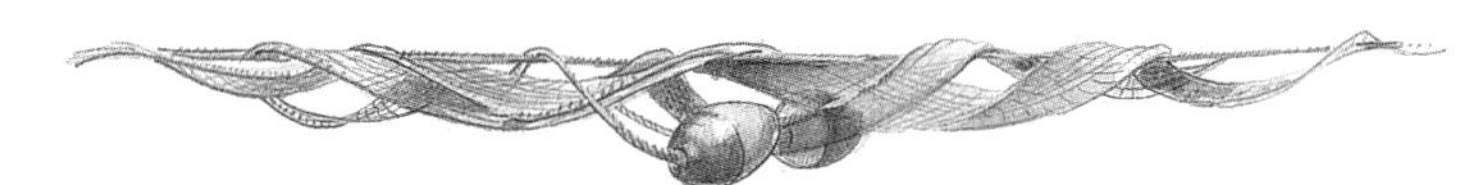

This recipe is based loosely on the Scandinavian tradition of gravlax, in which two whole fillets of salmon are cured with a blend of dill, sugar, and salt sandwiched between them, often with a splash of aquavit as well. My variation uses the martini-lover's favorite, gin, and I also add gin's main flavoring, juniper, for a wonderful depth of flavor. The color and crunch of lightly pickled red onion make a great finish to this appetizer.

Though just one salmon fillet piece is cured here, it still produces a generous amount, ideal for a cocktail party or other celebration. The cured salmon is also an optional element in other recipes, such as homemade bagels (page 28). Just be sure to plan ahead, since the salmon should cure for a minimum of 2 days (ideally 3) before serving. And don't forget to carefully remove all those pin bones before you begin, because they'll cause trouble later when you try to thinly slice the cured fish.

- ¼ cup coarse kosher or sea salt
- ¼ cup plus 1 tablespoon sugar
- 1 teaspoon crushed or coarsely ground white or black peppercorns
- 1 thick salmon fillet piece (about 2 pounds), skin on, pin bones removed
- ½ cup coarsely chopped flat-leaf (Italian) parsley
- 1 tablespoon coarsely chopped juniper berries
- 3 tablespoons gin
- ½ red onion
- ½ cup red wine vinegar
- Thinly sliced pumpernickel cocktail bread or toasted slices of baguette

Cut a piece of plastic wrap about 3 times as long as the salmon piece and lay the plastic in a shallow dish (such as a baking dish) so that the ends hang over evenly.

Combine the salt, ¼ cup of the sugar, and pepper in a small bowl and stir to mix. Scatter about one-quarter of this in the center of the plastic, over roughly the space that the fillet will cover. Set the salmon skin-side down on the plastic and scatter the parsley and juniper berries over. Drizzle with the gin and sprinkle the remaining salt-sugar mixture over the fish. Draw up the plastic wrap to fully enclose the salmon pieces. Top with another baking dish or small pan that will rest directly on the salmon. Add a few cans of food to weigh the salmon down and refrigerate for 2 to 3 days. If a good deal of liquid is building up in the packet, gently pierce the plastic to draw off that excess liquid into the dish.

An hour or so before you plan to serve the salmon, thinly slice the red onion and put it in a heatproof bowl. Add boiling water to just cover and let sit for 5 minutes, then drain.

While still warm (but well-drained), return the onion to the bowl and add the red wine vinegar and the remaining tablespoon of sugar with a pinch each of salt and pepper. Toss to mix until the sugar has dissolved. Let cool, stirring occasionally. When cool, drain off the vinegar and refrigerate the onions until ready to serve.

After the salmon has cured, discard the plastic wrap and scrape away the seasonings. Briefly pass the salmon under cold water to thoroughly rinse and pat dry well with paper towels. Using a sharp, slender knife, cut the salmon into paper-thin slices working at a near-horizontal angle.

Arrange the cured salmon on bread slices (halve the pieces crosswise first if quite large, or simply fold them over). Garnish with the pickled red onions and serve.

Makes about 12 to 16 servings

Herbed Salmon Sausages with Roasted Red Pepper Sauce

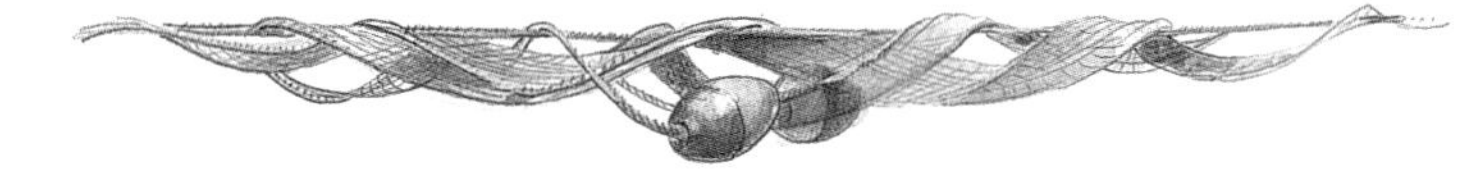

Feel free to alter the selection of herbs in this recipe to suit your taste and what might be in your garden. Chervil, dill, or basil would be good additions, but avoid strongly flavored herbs such as sage or oregano. A serving option for a cocktail party would be to set the individual slices of the salmon sausage on a cracker or small baguette slice, with a little dollop of the sauce on top. Any leftover sausage would be delicious alongside your scrambled eggs the next morning.

2 large red bell peppers
1½ pounds salmon fillet, skin and pin bones removed
1 egg
½ cup half-and-half
Salt and freshly ground white or black pepper
3 tablespoons minced chives
3 tablespoons minced flat-leaf (Italian) parsley
1 teaspoon minced thyme
1 tablespoon balsamic vinegar
Herb sprigs, for garnish

Roast the red peppers over a gas flame or under the broiler until the skin blackens, turning occasionally to roast evenly, about 10 minutes total. Put the peppers in a plastic bag, securely seal it, and set aside to cool. When cool enough to handle, peel away and discard the skin. Remove the core and seeds from the peppers and coarsely chop them.

Cut enough of the salmon into ¼-inch dice to make 1 cup; set aside. Cut the remaining salmon into larger pieces, put them in a food processor with the egg, and coarsely chop. Add the half-and-half with a good pinch each of salt and pepper and process until smooth. Transfer the mixture to a medium bowl and stir in the diced salmon along with half of the chives, half of the parsley, and half of the thyme.

Bring a few inches of water to a boil in a large, deep skillet or sauté pan over high heat. Drop in about 1 teaspoon of the mousse mixture and simmer until cooked through, about 1 minute. Taste the mousse, then adjust the seasoning in the remaining mousse if necessary.

Cut 4 pieces of foil about 12 inches long. Lightly brush the center of the foil with oil, leaving 2 inches free on each end. Spoon one-quarter of the salmon mousse down the center of each piece of foil. Wrap the foil around the mousse to form a cylinder about 1½ inches in diameter, twisting the ends gently to tighten and securely seal the cylinder.

Return the water to a boil over high heat. Add the mousse cylinders, reduce the heat to medium-low, and poach the sausages at a simmer, uncovered, for 20 minutes.

While the mousse is simmering, purée the roasted peppers in the food processor until smooth. Add the balsamic vinegar and the remaining chives, parsley, and thyme with salt and pepper to taste, pulsing to evenly blend. You may warm the sauce in a small pan over medium-low heat, if you like.

Lift the salmon packets from the water and carefully unwrap them over the sink, as water may have accumulated inside the foil. Cut each sausage into ¾-inch slices. Spoon the roasted pepper sauce onto individual plates, top with the sausage slices slightly overlapping in a circle. Add herb sprigs to the center and serve right away.

Makes 4 servings

Hot Artichoke and Salmon Dip

A salmon twist on that timeless classic crab and artichoke dip, this recipe is perfect for a buffet setting, or a cocktail party bite, particularly if you spoon the mixture onto crackers or toasted baguette slices for easy finger food. For some added spice, you could stir in a tablespoon or so of minced jalapeño chile before baking.

1 tablespoon vegetable oil
½ cup minced onion
8 ounces salmon fillet, skin and pin bones removed, finely diced
1 cup prepared mayonnaise
1 cup finely grated Parmesan cheese
1 can (14 ounces) artichoke hearts, drained, rinsed, and diced
Salt and freshly ground white or black pepper
2 tablespoons dried bread crumbs
Crackers and/or baguette slices, for serving

Heat the oil in a medium skillet over medium heat. Add the onion and cook, stirring often, until tender and aromatic, 2 to 3 minutes. Add the salmon and cook, stirring often, until it is just cooked through, 3 to 5 minutes. Transfer the mixture to a medium bowl and set aside to cool.

Preheat the oven to 400°F. Generously butter a 1-quart baking dish.

Add the mayonnaise, Parmesan cheese, and artichoke hearts to the bowl with the salmon. Season to taste with salt and pepper and stir well to thoroughly blend. Transfer the mixture to the prepared baking dish and sprinkle the bread crumbs evenly over. Bake until the mixture bubbles around the sides and the bread crumbs are lightly browned, 25 to 30 minutes.

To serve, set the baking dish on a large plate and surround the dish with crackers and/or baguette slices for scooping or spreading.

Makes 8 servings

Main Courses

Beer-Battered Salmon with Walla Walla Sweet Onion Rings

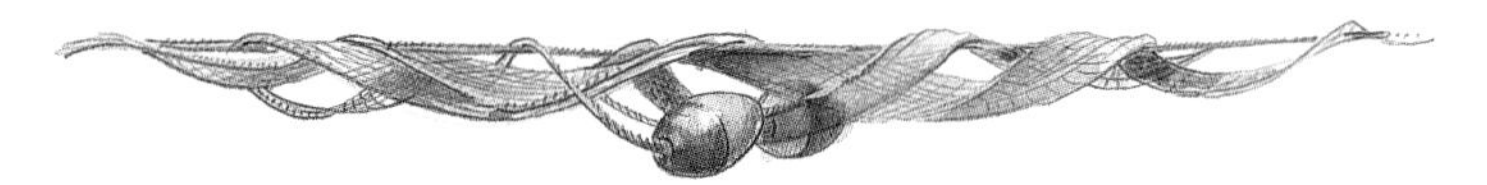

You may use another sweet onion, such as Maui or Vidalia, or even a standard yellow onion in place of the Walla Walla Sweet when they're not available. Or for a more classic fish-and-chips option, you could fry up some potatoes instead. Peel one large russet, cut into strips about ½ inch on each side, and soak in cold water for 30 minutes. Drain well and pat thoroughly dry with paper towels. Fry at 325°F until tender, 6 to 8 minutes, then drain and cool. Fry again at 375°F until nicely browned, a few minutes longer.

1½ pounds salmon fillet, skin and pin bones removed
Vegetable oil, for frying
1 large Walla Walla Sweet onion, cut into ¾-inch slices
Lemon wedges, for serving

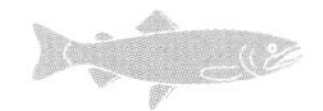

Tartar Sauce

1 cup top-quality mayonnaise, preferably homemade (page 41)
¼ cup finely chopped dill pickle
2 tablespoons minced shallot or onion
1 tablespoon minced flat-leaf (Italian) parsley
1 tablespoon white wine vinegar
2 teaspoons dill pickle juice
Salt and freshly ground white or black pepper

Beer Batter

1½ cups all-purpose flour
1½ teaspoons baking powder
½ teaspoon salt
¾ cup (1 12-ounce bottle) pale ale, more if needed

For the tartar sauce, combine the mayonnaise, pickle, shallot, parsley, vinegar, and pickle juice in a small bowl and stir well to blend. Season to taste with salt and pepper

and refrigerate until ready to serve, preferably at least 2 hours to allow the flavors to blend and develop.

Cut the salmon fillet into slices on the bias, about 1 inch thick. Separate the onion slices into individual rings.

Heat a few inches of oil to 375°F in a large, deep pot (the oil should not come more than halfway up the sides of the pot). Preheat the oven to 200°F.

While the oil is heating, make the batter. Combine the flour, baking powder, and salt in a medium bowl and whisk to mix. Whisk in the ale, adding a bit more if needed so that the batter has the consistency of heavy cream.

When the oil is heated, dip 4 or 5 of the onion rings into the batter and evenly coat, then lift up and allow excess to drip off. Carefully slip the rings into the hot oil and fry until nicely browned, 2 to 3 minutes. Scoop out the onion rings onto a brown paper- or paper towel-lined baking sheet, sprinkle lightly with salt, and keep warm in the oven. Continue with the remaining onion rings, allowing the oil to reheat between batches as needed.

Dip 3 or 4 salmon pieces into the batter, allowing excess to drip off, and slip them gently into the oil. Fry until browned and the salmon is just cooked through, about 3 minutes. Transfer to the tray with onion rings and repeat with the remaining salmon.

To serve, arrange the salmon pieces on individual plates with the onion rings alongside, add a generous dollop of the tartar sauce, and garnish with lemon wedges for squeezing.

Makes 4 servings

Walla Walla Sweets: While the Northwest touts many iconic foods that represent a distinct flavor of the region, few have the kind of recognition that Walla Walla Sweet onions do. In 1995, a federal USDA marketing order was enacted to protect the Walla Walla Sweet name. It designates a specific geographic region in which the official Walla Walla Sweet Onion moniker may be used, a small part of that region extending across the border into Oregon. This is reminiscent of the European practices that verify authentic regional foods—such as France's *appellation d'origine contrôlée* designation for everything from wine to sausage.

French soldier Peter Pieri is credited with bringing the seeds of an Italian sweet onion from Corsica to Walla Walla, Washington, in the late 1800s, where the community of Italian farmers helped spur the production of this distinctive sweet onion. The growing conditions proved ideal, the "sweetness" coming from a reduced level of sulfur in the onion, which leaves the onion tasting sweeter than similar yellow onions. Because these onions have a relatively high water content, they have a short shelf life, making Walla Walla Sweet onions a treat to enjoy while in season, through most of the summer.

Grilled Salmon Steaks with Israeli Couscous and Green Peas

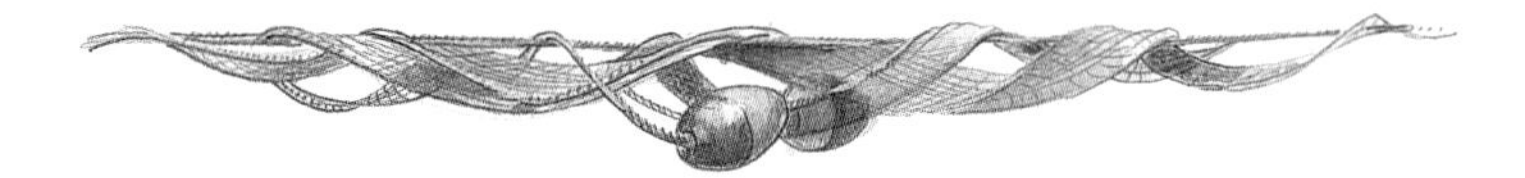

Israeli couscous, sometimes known as Middle Eastern couscous, is a much larger, pearl-like bead than the more common North African couscous that has a finer, more granular texture. Both are made from a flour-and-water dough, but the shape and size make for quite different results when cooked. You may use regular couscous if you like (follow cooking instructions on the package), or even a small pasta shape such as orzo.

1½ cups fresh shelled or frozen peas
¼ cup Israeli couscous
2 tablespoons extra virgin olive oil, plus more for the salmon
2 tablespoons water
1½ teaspoons chopped mint
Salt and freshly ground white or black pepper
4 salmon steaks (8 to 10 ounces each)

Preheat an outdoor grill.

Bring a medium saucepan of salted water to a boil over high heat. Add the peas to the boiling water and cook until just nearly tender and bright green, 1 to 2 minutes. Scoop them out with a slotted spoon, into a colander to drain. Return the water to a boil, add the couscous, and cook over medium heat until tender, 10 to 12 minutes. Drain the couscous well and return it to the saucepan.

Put ½ cup of the peas in a blender with the olive oil, water, mint, and a good pinch each of salt and pepper. Purée until smooth, then add the purée and the remaining whole peas to the pan with the couscous, stirring evenly to mix. Season to taste with salt and pepper and keep warm over low heat.

When the grill is hot, lightly rub the grill grate with oil. Rub the salmon steaks with extra virgin olive oil and season lightly with salt and pepper. Grill the salmon steaks until nicely browned on both sides and just a touch of translucence remains in the center, 3 to 5 minutes per side.

Set the grilled salmon steaks on individual plates, spoon the couscous and peas alongside, and serve right away.

Makes 4 servings

Brown Sugar-Glazed Salmon

Though I don't have much of a sweet tooth, this subtle mingling of salmon's richness with crunchy salt and the slightly caramel-molasses flavor of brown sugar does indeed make for a delicious combination. Add an optional drizzle of bourbon over the fish just after taking it off the grill for a spirited finish before serving. You may also simply bake the fillet in a 450°F oven when grilling isn't an option.

1 salmon fillet piece (about 2 pounds), skin on, pin bones removed

Coarse kosher salt or sea salt and freshly ground white or black pepper

¼ cup lightly packed light or dark brown sugar

Preheat an outdoor grill.

Cut a piece of foil just a bit larger than the salmon fillet and oil the foil. Set the salmon skin-side down on the foil and sprinkle the top with salt to your taste. Let sit until the grill is ready.

Just before putting the fish on the grill, spread the brown sugar evenly over the fish and season to taste with pepper. Put the fish on the grill, cover the grill, and cook, without turning the salmon, until just a touch of translucence remains in the center of the thickest part of the fish, 8 to 12 minutes for a thinner fillet piece, 15 to 18 minutes for a thicker fillet.

Carefully lift the fillet onto a platter or cutting board. Cut the salmon fillet into pieces to serve.

Makes 4 to 6 servings

Salmon and Saffron-Braised Fennel with Smoked Paprika Aïoli

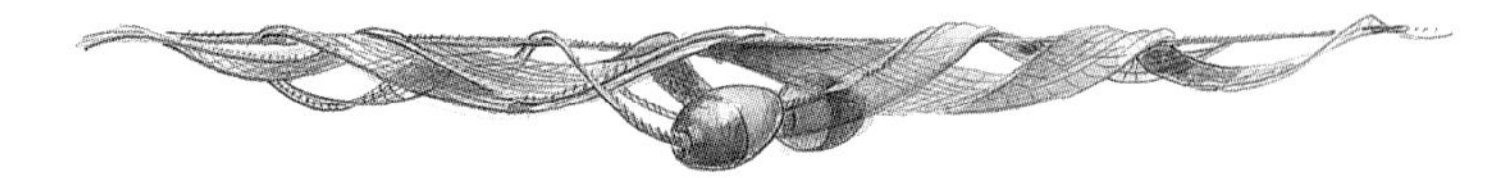

This recipe hints subtly at the aromatic bouillabaisse of Provence, with the flavorful elements of fennel, saffron, garlic, and a touch of Pastis. Smoked paprika is a highly flavorful and aromatic ingredient from Spain (where it goes by the name *pimenton de la vera*) that is quite unlike your average, mild paprika. Look for it in specialty food stores or spice markets, though you may use another type of paprika instead.

2 large fennel bulbs
2 tablespoons olive oil
½ cup salmon stock (page 37), fish stock, or water
2 tablespoons plus 1½ teaspoons Pastis or other anise liqueur
1 large pinch saffron threads, steeped in 2 tablespoons warm water
1 teaspoon minced garlic
4 salmon fillet pieces (6 to 8 ounces each), pin bones removed

Smoked Paprika Aïoli

1 egg yolk
1 tablespoon white wine vinegar
2 cloves garlic, crushed or finely chopped
¾ cup olive oil (not extra virgin)
½ teaspoon smoked paprika
Salt and freshly ground white or black pepper

For the smoked paprika aïoli, combine the egg yolk, vinegar, and garlic in a food processor and pulse to blend. With the blades running, begin adding the oil a drop or two at a time until the yolk mixture starts to thicken, showing that an emulsion is beginning to form. Continue adding the oil in a thin, steady stream. When all the oil has been added, add the smoked paprika with salt and pepper to taste and pulse a few more times to evenly mix. Transfer the aïoli to a bowl, cover with plastic wrap, and refrigerate until ready to serve. The aïoli will have a more pronounced flavor if made a couple of hours before serving.

Preheat the oven to 375°F. Line a baking dish with a piece of foil and lightly oil the foil.

Trim the stalks from the fennel bulbs and pick off some tender fennel fronds to use as garnish. Halve and core the fennel bulbs and cut them with the grain into ¼-inch slices.

Heat the olive oil in a large skillet over medium heat. Add the fennel with a good pinch of salt and sauté until beginning to soften, 5 minutes, stirring often. Add the stock, 2 tablespoons of the Pastis, the saffron and its soaking liquid, and the garlic and stir to evenly mix. Reduce the heat to medium-low and cook gently until the fennel is just tender and the liquid is reduced by about three-quarters, about 15 minutes.

Meanwhile, drizzle the remaining 1½ teaspoons of the Pastis over the salmon pieces and rub with your fingers to evenly coat. Season the salmon with salt and pepper and set the pieces on the prepared baking dish. Bake the salmon until just a touch of translucence remains in the center of the thickest part, 6 to 10 minutes.

To serve, transfer the baked salmon pieces to individual plates (with or without the skin, as you prefer) and spoon the braised fennel with some of its cooking liquids alongside. Top the salmon with a generous dollop of the smoked paprika aïoli and a tuft of fennel fronds. Serve right away.

Makes 4 servings

Grilled Whole Salmon Dad's Way

My dad was not a big cook, though he sure did love a good meal. Like many American men, his culinary domain was out-of-doors, whether cooking breakfast over a campfire on hiking trips or presiding over the backyard grill. Our "grill" was actually a well-used ceramic kamado oven brought back from Japan, my birthplace and my father's last overseas tour of Navy duty before the family returned to the Seattle area. His *pièce de résistance* grilling contribution was whole salmon—done simply, as is best with such a glorious fish. Partly wrapped in foil, the flesh's maximum moisture is preserved while some of that smoky essence from the charcoal embers embellishes the flavor. It was the showstopper for special dinners or to wow out-of-town visitors with our great local eats.

It's not always easy to find whole head-on salmon (best to call ahead to your local fish market), as the head will generally begin spoiling faster than the flesh and it also adds to bulk for transport. But head-on grilled salmon will retain a maximum of flavor and moisture, plus the added bonus of those two delectable salmon cheeks at which the chef gets first dibs. An optional sauce to serve with the salmon would be the watercress sauce on page 52.

2 cups wood smoking chips (optional)
6 tablespoons unsalted butter, melted
1 whole salmon (about 5 to 7 pounds), head and tail intact, cleaned and scaled
Salt and freshly ground white or black pepper
½ medium onion, thinly sliced
2 large lemons (1 thinly sliced and 1 juiced)
1 lime, thinly sliced
Small handful flat-leaf (Italian) parsley sprigs

Preheat an outdoor grill. Soak the smoking chips, if using, in a bowl of cold water.

Cut a piece of heavy-duty foil about 2½ times as long as the fish. Drizzle a tablespoon or two of the melted butter lengthwise down the center of the foil. Set the salmon on top of the butter. Season the belly of the fish with salt and pepper, then add the onion slices, lemon slices, and lime slices, distributing them evenly. Finally, add the parsley sprigs to the belly. Add the lemon juice to the remaining melted butter, stir well, and drizzle this over the surface of the fish.

Fold the ends of the foil up over the fish to meet in the center. Crimp the foil along the long side edges so they're well sealed without too snugly enclosing the fish. At the top center, where the foil ends meet, fold back to make a loose opening, making sure the sides remain sealed to hold in the juices during cooking.

When the grill is hot, if using a charcoal grill, spread the coals out in an even layer. Drain the smoking chips and scatter them over the coals (if using a gas grill, follow the manufacturer's instructions). Carefully set the salmon packet in the center of the grill grate, cover the grill, and cook until only a slight hint of translucence remains in the center of the thickest part (gently pull back some of the foil and poke into the flesh with the tip of a small knife to check), 20 to 30 minutes. Lift the salmon packet onto a heatproof platter, fold back the foil so that the cooking liquids are retained. Serve right away.

Makes 8 to 12 servings

Sesame-Crusted Salmon Steaks with Wasabi Butter

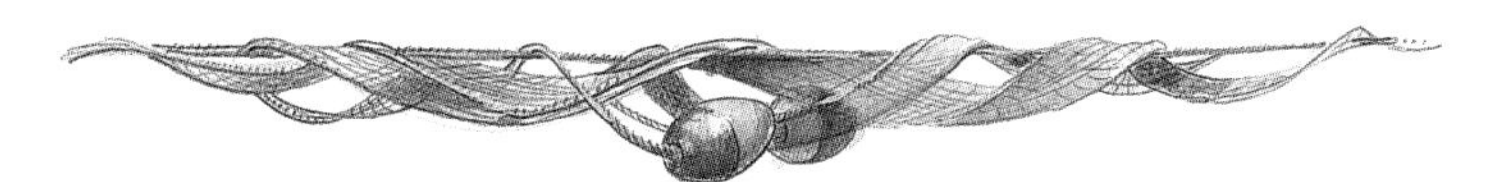

Fresh wasabi is not widely available (though it is grown in the Northwest), but can be found on occasion at Asian greengrocers and specialty food markets. Grate it as you would ginger, on a nubbed porcelain grater or with a fine Microplane-style grater. In place of fresh wasabi, you may use 1 tablespoon wasabi powder stirred with 1 tablespoon water.

Shichimi togarashi is a Japanese spice blend that typically includes crushed red pepper flakes, dried nori, sesame seed, dried orange peel, and other pungent ingredients—a little goes a long way. *Togarashi* is available in Asian markets and well-stocked grocery stores.

¼ cup unsalted butter, at room temperature
1 tablespoon freshly grated wasabi
½ teaspoon soy sauce
Salt
4 salmon steaks (about 8 ounces each)
1 teaspoon sesame oil
½ teaspoon *shichimi togarashi* or pinch freshly ground white or black pepper
2 teaspoons white sesame seeds
2 tablespoons vegetable oil

Combine the butter and wasabi in a small bowl and stir with a fork to evenly blend. Add the soy sauce and a pinch of salt and stir until well mixed. Transfer the wasabi butter to a piece of plastic wrap and form it into a short cylinder about 1 inch across, twisting the ends of the plastic to help form a firm cylinder. Refrigerate until ready to serve, at least 1 hour.

Rub the salmon steaks with the sesame oil and season both sides lightly with the *shichimi togarashi* and salt. Scatter the sesame seeds evenly, but not too heavily, on one side of each salmon steak.

Heat the vegetable oil in a large skillet, preferably nonstick, over medium heat. Add the salmon steaks, sesame seed–side down, and cook until the seeds are lightly toasted, 3 to 4 minutes. Turn the steaks and continue cooking until there is just a touch of translucence in the center of the salmon, about 5 minutes longer.

To serve, set the salmon steaks on individual plates. Unwrap the wasabi butter and cut it into 4 even slices. Top each steak with a slice of butter and serve right away.

Makes 4 servings

Kodiak Salmon Pirog with Dilled Sour Cream

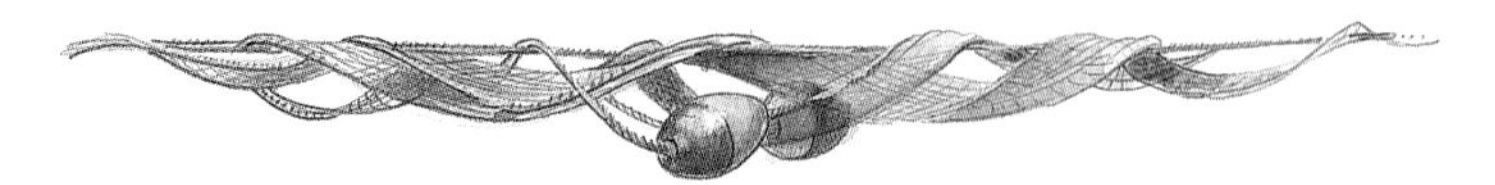

While editor of *Simply Seafood* magazine, I made a most memorable summertime trip to Alaska's Kodiak Island to spend time with salmon fishing families at the southern edge of the island, near the tiny village of Akhiok. A highlight of the week was a potluck feast that included—little surprise—salmon cooked a couple dozen ways. On the groaning table were a few variations on the Russian-inspired pirog, a savory fish pie that is testament to the heritage that the Last Frontier shares with Russia, its nearest neighbor to the west.

2 tablespoons vegetable oil
½ small head (about ½ pound) green cabbage, trimmed and finely shredded
4 tablespoons water
2 tablespoons minced flat-leaf (Italian) parsley
4 teaspoons minced dill
Salt and freshly ground white or black pepper
1 pound mushrooms, wiped clean and very finely chopped
1 cup finely chopped onion
1½ pounds salmon fillet, skin and pin bones removed
1 egg
1½ cups cooked long grain white rice
½ cup sour cream
1 tablespoon freshly squeezed lemon juice

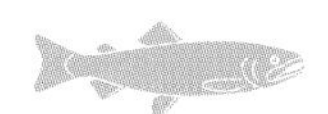

Pastry

3 cups all-purpose flour
1 teaspoon salt
¾ cup unsalted butter, cut into pieces and chilled
1 tablespoon freshly squeezed lemon juice
5 to 6 tablespoons ice water

For the pastry, combine the flour and salt in a food processor and pulse once to blend. Add the chilled butter pieces and pulse until the butter is finely chopped and the flour mixture has a coarse sandy texture. Add the lemon juice, pulse once, and then add the water 1 tablespoon at a time, pulsing once or twice after each addition. It's important not to overmix the dough or it will be tough rather than flaky. (Alternatively, combine the flour and salt in a large bowl and cut in the butter with a pastry cutter or two table knives until it has a coarse sandy texture. Add the lemon juice and water, and stir with a fork to mix, adding more water if needed.) Turn the dough out onto a work surface and form it into 2 equal balls. Wrap the dough in plastic and refrigerate for at least 30 minutes before rolling it out.

Meanwhile, heat 1 tablespoon of the oil in a large skillet over medium heat. Add the shredded cabbage with 2 tablespoons of the water and cook, stirring often, until very tender and excess liquid has evaporated, 8 to 10 minutes. Stir in 1 tablespoon of the parsley with 1 teaspoon of the dill and season the cabbage to taste with salt and pepper. Set aside in a bowl and wipe out the skillet. Heat the remaining 1 tablespoon of the oil in the skillet. Add the mushrooms and onion and cook over medium-high heat, stirring often, until the mushrooms are tender and the liquid that they give off has evaporated, 5 to 7 minutes. Season the mushrooms to taste with salt and pepper and add the remaining 1 tablespoon of the parsley with another 1 teaspoon of the dill. Set aside to cool.

Preheat the oven to 375°F. Line a large baking sheet with parchment paper or foil.

Cut the salmon fillet across into slices about ½ inch thick. Lightly beat the egg in a small bowl with the remaining 2 tablespoons of the water and a pinch of salt to make an egg wash for the pastry.

Roll out 1 ball of the pastry to a rectangle about 10 inches wide and 14 inches long, trimming the edges to neaten them. Set the pastry on the prepared baking sheet and lightly brush some of the egg wash evenly over the pastry base. Leaving a 1-inch border free around the edge, spread the cooked rice on the pastry, then spoon the shredded cabbage evenly over. Lay the salmon slices on top of the cabbage, cutting and rearranging the pieces as needed so the salmon evenly covers the cabbage. Season the salmon lightly with salt and pepper, then spread the mushroom mixture evenly over the salmon.

Roll out the remaining dough to a rectangle about 12 inches wide and 16 inches long, trimming the edges to neaten them. Lay this pastry over the filling, lining up the edges with the pastry base as much as possible and very gently stretching the dough a bit if needed. Press firmly on the edges to seal them, trim with a small knife to neaten, then use your fingers or the tines of a fork to crimp and seal the edges well. If you have any pastry trimmings left, cut them into strips or decorative shapes and arrange them on top of the pastry, if you like. Brush the pastry top with egg wash and use kitchen shears or the tip of a sharp knife to cut a few vents in the top to allow steam to escape during cooking.

Bake the pirog until the pastry is well browned, 30 to 40 minutes. While the pirog is baking, stir together the sour cream, lemon juice, and remaining 2 teaspoons of the dill. Refrigerate until ready to serve.

Take the pirog from the oven and let sit for about 5 minutes before cutting into pieces to serve. Arrange the pirog on individual plates, spoon some of the dilled sour cream alongside, and serve right away.

Makes 8 servings

Yukon River Salmon: Pomp and Subsistence

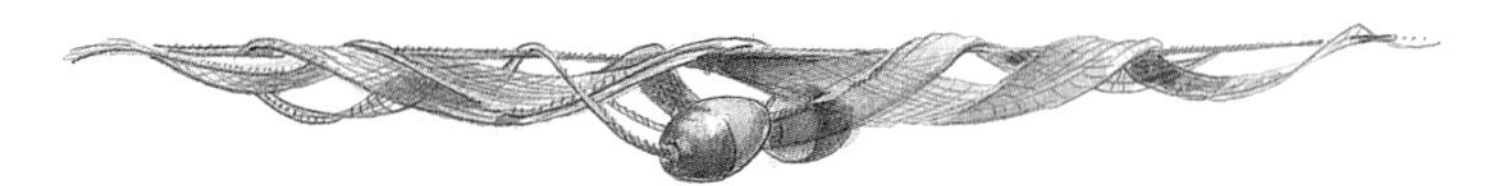

A salmon by any other name may taste as sweet, but some salmon do stand out from the crowd of these delicious fish. The "pomp" in this case is the recent media and consumer delight over the first salmon from Alaska's Yukon River sent to the Lower 48 in quite some time. For three decades the fish was so highly prized by the price-no-object Japanese that virtually all of the Yukon commercial harvest headed directly across the Pacific. There it was steamed, dried, and flaked to use as a sort of condiment. But economic and cultural changes in Japan have reduced their interest in these fish. The return of the Yukon River salmon to Lower 48 markets and restaurant menus made a big splash, touted in Northwest papers and even garnering a profile in the *New York Times* (complete with a photo of me holding a huge Yukon River king).

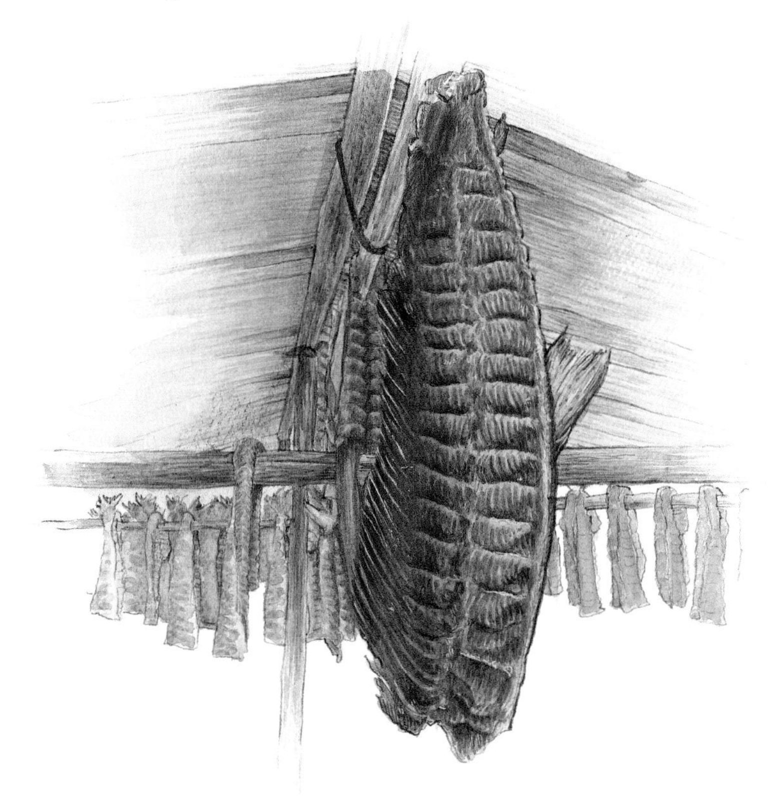

While the domestic commercial value of these salmon is increasing, it's the value of the subsistence fishing that remains paramount. Subsistence is a term that applies seldom to our lives today. For me, it basically means making sure I don't run out of milk, and then it's just a five-minute drive to the store to remedy the situation. The hunter-gatherer element of our genetic makeup is but a distant memory for most of us. But despite the fact that their lives, too, are changing in this 21st century, Alaska Native people still continue the age-old tradition of harvesting and preserving the bounty of native foods available, to sustain them throughout the year to come.

I had the cherished opportunity to learn more about this ritual when visiting fish camps of the Yup'ik people along the Yukon River in far north Alaska. At one camp we visited with Lily, her father Johnny, and mother Marcia, among other family members. Lily, one of 10 children in her family, has been coming to this same camp since the age of 10, over four decades ago. She said that her large family planned to catch about 200 king salmon that season for their subsistence needs, nearly all of which will be dried, smoked, salted, and preserved in jars. The fish already caught had been filleted so that the bones were removed and the tail held the two fillet portions together. The flesh of the fillets was slashed nearly to the skin, exposing maximum surface area to dry and cure as quickly and evenly as possible. First dried outside, under tarps, until the flesh was no longer moist to the touch, the fish then went into smoke shacks where cottonwood or alder wood fires glowed with low embers.

Having visited the villages of Emmonak and Kotlik, it's easy to understand how valuable the subsistence traditions still are. They may have satellite TV and outboard motors, but neither alters the fact that they are still incredibly remote. Everything in those towns came in by boat or plane; no road system connects them with other towns. Kotlik has a network of boardwalks for ATV and foot traffic only, and Emmonak's few roads are populated by some well-worn vehicles that originally came in by barge.

Everyone I spoke with about these fish camp traditions said that they see no chance of the practice waning in the face of modern times. In a Pacific Coast Native setting in British Columbia, I saw another camp, called Kyel ("Seaweed Camp") where Gitga'at Indian Darryl goes with his family every May to harvest and dry seaweed and halibut. Darryl explained the fish camp traditions to me as a "cycle that can't be broken. It's important for the children to learn and important for the elders to share what they know." So, the succession of generations will continue to pass on subsistence traditions well into the future.

Crispy Salmon with Sorrel Cream Sauce

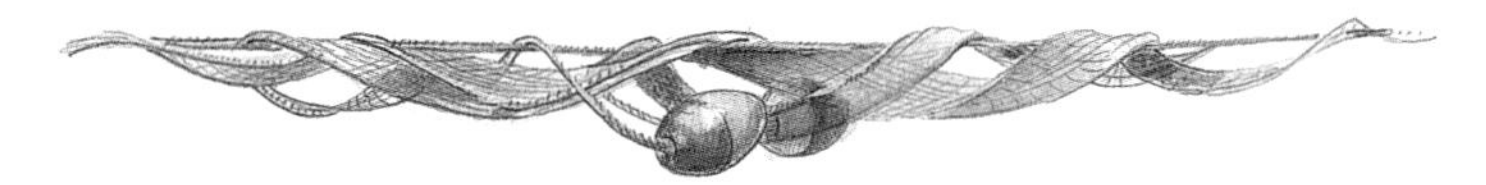

Sorrel is an underappreciated green in this country, though a staple in France and other parts of Europe. The leaves naturally cook into a thick purée (rather than holding their shape as look-alike spinach leaves do) and turn an unfortunate Army green, but sorrel packs a wonderful lemony-herbal flavor that's ideal alongside salmon or roasted chicken. I adore it. The puckery green also adds fresh zip to salads and makes a delicious creamed soup, perhaps paired with spinach to help amend its color.

The pan-frying method here cooks the fish just on the skin side, without turning, so the skin gets nicely browned and crisp while the surface remains tender and moist. Even if you're not usually a fan of eating salmon skin, this may change your mind. Be sure the salmon skin is scaleless, though.

4 salmon fillet pieces (6 to 8 ounces each), skin on, pin bones removed
2 tablespoons olive oil

Sorrel Cream Sauce

2 tablespoons unsalted butter
¼ cup finely chopped shallot or onion
½ cup dry white wine
¾ cup heavy cream or crème fraîche
8 ounces sorrel, rinsed and dried
Salt and freshly ground white or black pepper

For the sorrel cream sauce, heat the butter in a small saucepan over medium heat. Add the shallot and cook, stirring, until tender and aromatic, 2 to 3 minutes. Add the wine and bring to a boil over high heat, then return to medium and simmer until reduced by about half, 3 to 5 minutes. Add half of the cream and reduce again by about half, 2 to 3 minutes longer.

While the cream is reducing, remove any tough stems from the sorrel and cut the leaves into thin shreds. Don't worry about cutting the leaves individually: I usually compress a generous handful under my fingers and carefully cut across the pile into more or less even strips. Add the sorrel to the saucepan and stir over medium-low heat until it is wilted and forms a thick, almost smooth purée, 12 to 15 minutes. Season the sauce to taste with salt and pepper and keep warm over low heat while cooking the salmon.

Season the salmon pieces with salt and pepper. Heat the oil in a large skillet, preferably nonstick, over medium-high heat. Add the salmon pieces, skin-side down, and partly cover the skillet with its lid or a piece of foil (you want to be sure the steam from cooking escapes or the skin won't crisp up as it should). Cook until the skin is nicely browned and crisp and just a touch of translucence remains on the surface of the fish, 6 to 10 minutes.

To serve, stir the remaining cream into the sorrel sauce and warm through. Set the salmon pieces on individual plates and spoon the sorrel cream sauce partly over and alongside the fish. Serve right away.

Makes 4 servings

Yukon River King Salmon with Olmstead Orchards Rainier Cherries, Broken Balsamic Reduction, and Smoky Almond Beurre Noisette

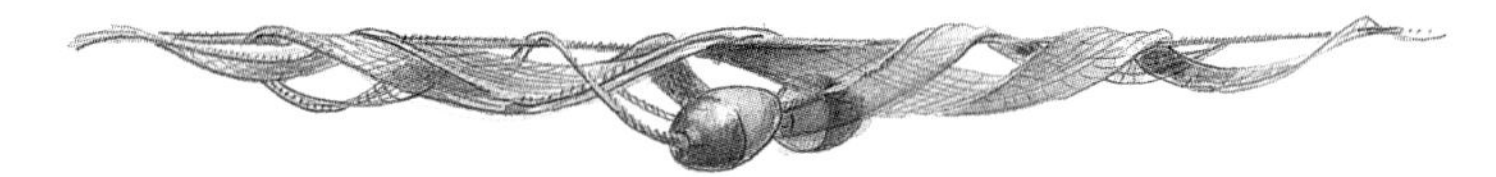

This recipe was made with the glorious Yukon River king salmon in mind, its rich flavor ideally complemented by the fresh sweet cherries and smoky-nutty quality of the garnish. You may certainly use other fresh wild salmon in its place. The recipe is the creation of executive chef Kevin Davis at The Oceanaire Seafood Room in downtown Seattle, where he works wonders with the best of whatever seafood is available seasonally. He's a big fan of the blush Rainier cherries from Olmstead Orchards in Grandview, Washington, which begin to appear just about the time that Yukon River king salmon does—mid June. The combined flavors are a match made in heaven.

Note that the pale flesh of Rainier cherries will begin to brown very soon after they are pitted. It is best to pit the cherries just before they are needed.

¼ cup balsamic vinegar
2 tablespoons extra virgin olive oil
4 tablespoons unsalted butter
¼ cup sliced shallot
¼ cup coarsely chopped smoked almonds
1 teaspoon finely grated orange zest
1 teaspoon minced rosemary
8 to 10 ounces Rainier cherries or other sweet cherry, pitted
Salt and freshly ground white or black pepper
4 salmon fillet pieces (6 to 8 ounces each), skin and pin bones removed
2 teaspoons olive oil
Opal basil or other basil leaves, for garnish

Preheat an outdoor grill.

Put the vinegar in a small saucepan and bring to a boil over medium-high heat. Reduce the heat to medium and simmer until the vinegar is reduced by about half, 3 to 5 minutes. Take the pan from the heat and set aside to cool. Add the extra virgin olive oil and blend with a fork; set aside.

Melt the butter in a medium skillet over medium-high heat until it turns a medium brown and has a nutty aroma (known as *beurre noisette*, or "nut brown butter"), 1 to 2 minutes. Add the shallot, almonds, orange zest, and rosemary and toss quickly just until the shallots are tender and the mixture is aromatic, 1 to 2 minutes. Take the skillet from the heat and add the cherries, tossing quickly to coat with the other ingredients. Season to taste with salt and pepper and set aside.

Brush the salmon pieces lightly with the olive oil and season with salt and pepper. When the grill is hot, lightly rub the grill grate with oil and grill the salmon until just a touch of translucence remains in the center, 3 to 5 minutes per side.

To serve, spoon some of the cherry mixture into the center of individual plates, moving the cherries themselves to the outer edge. Set the grilled salmon pieces in the center and top with the basil for garnish. Stir the balsamic-oil mixture with a spoon and drizzle it around the salmon on each plate. Serve right away.

Makes 4 servings

Lemon Pasta Alfredo with Salmon

For a more pronounced salmon flavor, you could replace the fresh salmon with 8 ounces of flaked smoked salmon, which also streamlines the recipe to make it super-quick—just the thing for a busy weeknight dinner.

While large lemons have great visual appeal and are preferable when you need pretty slices to show off, I usually choose smaller lemons for cooking. Not only are they less expensive, but the yield of juice they provide is generally better than that of the larger lemons, which often have a thick skin and less juicy flesh for their size.

¾ pound salmon fillet, skin and pin bones removed
2 small lemons
¾ cup half-and-half or heavy cream
2 tablespoons unsalted butter
Salt and freshly ground white or black pepper
¾ pound dried or fresh fettuccine
½ cup freshly grated Parmesan cheese, plus more for serving

Bring a large pot of generously salted water to a boil for cooking the pasta. While the water is heating, cut the salmon fillet into ½-inch dice. Grate enough zest from one of the lemons to make 1 teaspoon and squeeze the juice from both lemons.

Combine the half-and-half and butter in a medium skillet and bring to a boil over medium-high heat. Reduce the heat to medium and simmer until slightly thickened, about 3 minutes (less if using heavy cream). Add the diced salmon, lemon juice, and lemon zest and cook, stirring gently to separate the salmon, until the fish has just a touch of translucence remaining in the center, 2 to 3 minutes. Season to taste with salt and pepper and set the skillet aside.

When the water is at a rolling boil, add the pasta and stir for a few seconds to help separate the strands. Boil until al dente, 1 to 2 minutes for fresh pasta, 7 to 10 minutes for dried pasta. Drain the pasta well, shaking it in a colander to remove all excess water. Add the pasta to the skillet with the sauce, sprinkle the Parmesan over, and carefully toss to evenly mix.

Arrange the pasta on individual plates, sprinkle a bit more Parmesan cheese over, and serve right away.

Makes 4 to 6 servings

Broiled Salmon Steaks with Cranberry Compote

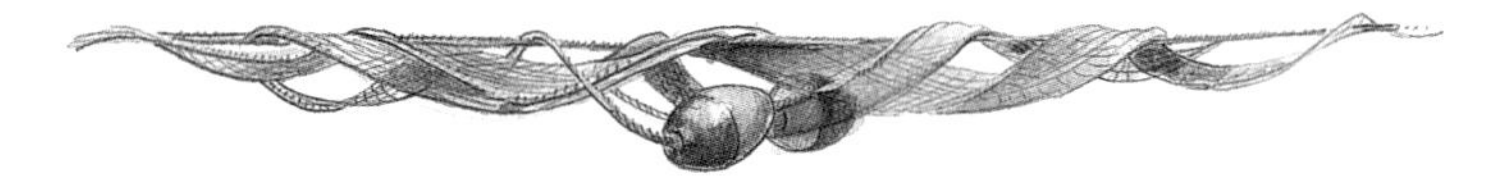

The tang of cranberries pairs beautifully with the richness of salmon, and the deep ruby color of the berries plays well off the fish's hue. During the summer months when other fresh berries are available, try using blackberries or blueberries in place of the cranberries, adding sugar only if necessary.

1 tablespoon vegetable oil
1 medium onion, finely chopped
1 bag (12 ounces) fresh cranberries
1 tart apple, peeled, cored, and chopped
¼ cup water
3 tablespoons sugar, more to taste
1 tablespoon red wine vinegar, more to taste
4 salmon steaks or boneless, skinless fillet pieces (6 to 8 ounces each)
Salt and freshly ground white or black pepper

Heat the oil in a medium saucepan over medium heat. Add the onion and cook until tender and aromatic, about 5 minutes. Stir in the cranberries, apple, water, sugar, and

Northwest Cranberries: As most Americans know, the Pilgrims were introduced to the local cranberry by Native Americans on the East Coast (hence the cranberry sauce on our Thanksgiving tables). The same happened here on the West Coast, too. The bogs in Grayland, Washington, in the heart of the "Cranberry Coast," were started by Finnish farmers 150 years ago. Fresh berries will keep for months, which is a good thing as they are only harvested from mid-October to mid-November (buy an extra bag or two at the holidays and toss them in the freezer).

There is a cranberry museum on Washington's Long Beach Peninsula where you can learn about cranberry farming and its history in the Pacific Northwest, in the region where you can see the cranberry blossoms in May and watch the harvest in October. The Furford Cranberry Museum in nearby Grayland, Washington, has a collection of old cranberry growing equipment. Grayland also hosts an annual Cranberry Festival in October, and Bandon, Oregon, hosts one every September.

vinegar. Cover the pan and cook, stirring occasionally, until the mixture begins to thicken, about 15 minutes. Do not boil or the berries will cook to a purée; reduce the heat to medium-low if needed. Season to taste with salt, pepper, and additional sugar and/or vinegar to taste.

Preheat the broiler. Line a baking sheet with foil and lightly oil the foil.

Season each side of the salmon pieces with salt and pepper and spread about 1 tablespoon of the compote on the top of each. Set the steaks compote-side up on the prepared baking sheet. Broil the salmon about 4 inches below the heat for 3 to 4 minutes, turn the salmon and spread another tablespoon of compote on them. Broil until just a touch of translucence remains in the center of the fish at the thickest part, 3 to 4 minutes longer. Meanwhile, reheat the remaining compote.

Transfer the salmon to individual plates, spoon the cranberry compote partly over and alongside, and serve immediately.

Makes 4 servings

Herb-Tattooed Salmon with Tomato-Herb Salad

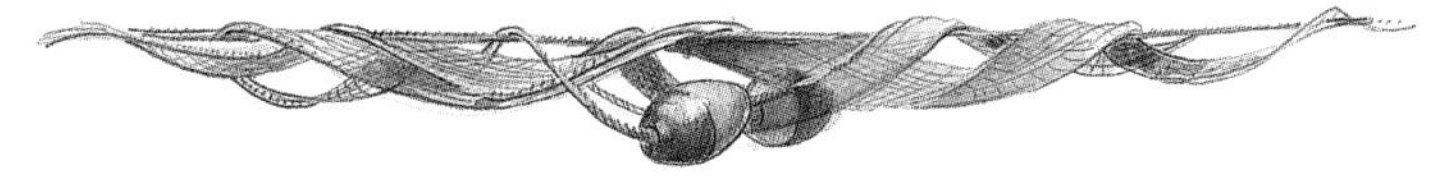

This dish is particularly delicious in late summer when flavorful heirloom tomatoes are available. A variety of different cherry tomatoes or other small tomatoes—halved or left whole depending on their size—will make for a particularly striking presentation.

4 salmon fillet pieces (6 to 8 ounces each), skin on, pin bones removed
2 tablespoons vegetable oil
Small handful tender, small herb leaves (chervil, flat-leaf parsley, tarragon, and/or basil)

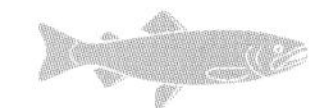

Tomato-Herb Salad

2 tablespoons herb vinegar or white wine vinegar
1 tablespoon minced shallot or onion
Salt and freshly ground white or black pepper
4 tablespoons extra virgin olive oil
8 to 10 ounces tomatoes, preferably heirloom, cored and coarsely chopped
2 tablespoons minced herbs (chervil, flat-leaf parsley, tarragon, chives, and/or basil)

For the tomato-herb salad, combine the vinegar, shallot, and a good pinch of salt in a small bowl and whisk to blend. Set aside until the salt is dissolved, about 5 minutes. Slowly pour in the olive oil, whisking constantly. Add the tomatoes and herbs, toss gently to coat, and set aside while cooking the fish.

Set the salmon pieces skin-side down on the work surface. Lay the herb leaves in an attractive pattern on the flesh side of the salmon, not covering it completely but creating a nice contrast of color. Press down with your fingers to help the herbs stick, then season the fish lightly with salt and pepper.

Heat the oil in a large skillet, preferably nonstick, over medium-high heat. Carefully add the salmon pieces, herb-side down, and sauté without disturbing until the flesh is lightly browned, about 2 minutes. Turn the fish pieces and reduce the heat to medium. Continue cooking until the skin is browned and there is just a touch of translucence in the center of the thickest portion of the flesh, 4 to 7 minutes.

Transfer the salmon to individual plates. Spoon the tomato salad partly over and alongside the salmon, drizzling any remaining dressing over the fish. Serve right away.

Makes 4 servings

Steamed Ginger Salmon with Mushrooms

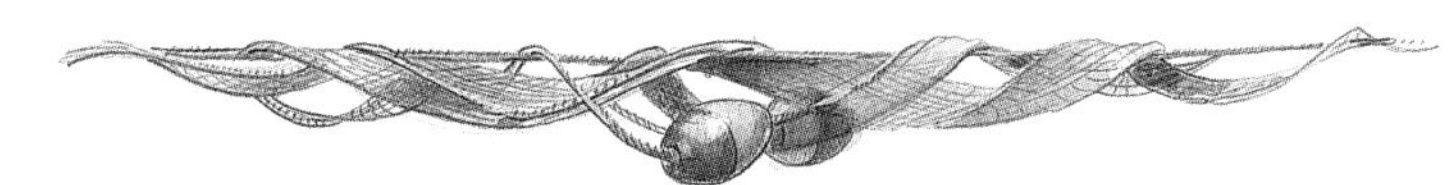

Steaming is a perfect way to blend rich salmon with the aromatic ingredients from the Pacific Rim. One such ingredient is lemongrass, a tall, stiff stalk that has a distinctive herbal-lemon aroma and flavor. Look for it in Asian markets or well-stocked grocery stores. Peel away a few of the outer layers and use only the more tender core at the base of the stalk.

4 salmon fillet pieces (6 to 8 ounces each), skin and pin bones removed
2 tablespoons sake or dry white wine
2 tablespoons soy sauce
1 teaspoon chili paste or ½ teaspoon hot pepper sauce
1 teaspoon rice vinegar
½ teaspoon sesame oil
3 green onions, trimmed and both white and green portions thinly sliced on the bias
1 tablespoon slivered ginger
2 cloves garlic, minced
1 teaspoon minced lemongrass (about 1 stalk)
8 ounces mixed fresh mushrooms (oyster mushrooms, shiitakes, and/or button mushrooms), brushed clean, trimmed, and thinly sliced
Cilantro sprigs, for garnish

Lightly score the salmon pieces 3 or 4 times on both sides with the tip of a sharp knife, in shallow, diagonal cuts. Put the fish on a heatproof platter or plate(s) that will fit in your steamer. In a small bowl, combine the sake, soy sauce, chili paste, rice vinegar, and sesame oil. Pour the mixture over the fish, turning once or twice to evenly coat the salmon. Scatter the green onions, ginger, garlic, and lemongrass over the fish. Top with the mushrooms in an even layer.

In a wok or deep pot, bring a few inches of water to a boil. Put the platter or plates of fish on a steamer tray (or 2), cover, and set the baskets over the boiling water. Steam until just a touch of translucence remains at the center of the thickest part of the salmon, 6 to 10 minutes.

Carefully remove the plates from the steamer and transfer the fish and mushrooms to individual plates. Drizzle some of the cooking liquids over, garnish with cilantro sprigs, and serve right away.

Makes 4 servings

Cooking Northwest Wild Salmon

Buying and Storing Salmon

One rule when choosing fish, almost without exception, is that it should never smell "fishy," an unfortunate adjective that doesn't do justice to the clean, fresh aroma of top-quality fish. When buying salmon, whether whole, fillet, or steak, the fish should have a subtle aroma of the brisk seaside air at high tide, not at all pungent. Any hint of an ammonia-like aroma is a telltale sign of old age.

We don't see much whole, head-on salmon in markets today, unless you're buying direct from fishermen or in a specialty seafood shop. On whole fish, look for the eyes to be clear, not cloudy, and not sunken in, which indicates a fish beyond its prime. Gills should be moist and have a bright red color; brick-brown color means a fish too long out of the water and not well chilled. If the whole fish has had its head removed, check the head end to see that the flesh is not dried out or discolored.

With any pieces of salmon, the flesh should be firm and spring back when gently pressed; if you press your finger gently into the salmon and it makes a permanent indentation, the flesh is not very fresh.

The flesh should have generally even color tones, no blotches of brown or yellow showing deterioration. Note, however, that between the flesh and skin of salmon is a distinct layer of fatty flesh that's brownish-gray and is naturally so. This layer has a stronger flavor than the rest of the flesh and some people prefer to remove it before eating, though most salmon fans enjoy it.

When storing salmon, keep it well chilled right up to the time that you cook it. Typically the back of the lowest shelf in your refrigerator is the coldest spot. Ideally you will cook salmon within a day or two of purchasing it. I don't recommend freezing salmon at home—especially previously frozen fish—unless you have a freezer that reaches at least -10°F (see page 34). If the store is selling previously frozen fish and you're interested in buying some to cook down the line, ask whether they have some of that fish still frozen so you can take it quickly home and pop it in your freezer.

Preparing Salmon

Scaling, filleting, and even skinning whole fillets usually can be done for you at full-service seafood counters, to save you some work at home. But just so you're prepared, here are the basics.

Removing scales is the biggest chore and should only be a consideration on whole fish, though many markets will have already scaled the fish before setting it out. Scales are tiny, bony plates that are layered, overlapping, something like roof tiles (and with much the same role of protection) on fish skin from the head toward the tail of the fish. To remove scales, you need to scrape them off in the opposite direction, from tail to head. There are special tools made just for this task, but I scale fish seldom enough that the back of a heavy kitchen knife is sufficient. Beware, though, that the scales will fly randomly all over the place. Do this outside on a newspaper-covered table for easier clean up.

Describing how to fillet and skin a fish with words rather than pictures is probably like doing the same for square dancing. But here it goes. If the head is still attached, first make a downward cut just behind the gills halfway through the fish, until the blade meets the backbone. Then begin with a long, smooth stroke of the knife along the back of the fish, working with the blade of the knife about parallel to the work surface. Continue making these long, smooth strokes, following the backbone from head to tail end, sliding the blade of the knife along the backbone and ribs. At the tail end, make another perpendicular cut down to separate the fillet from the tail. Turn the fish over and repeat on the second side, which is a bit trickier than on the first side, with less support underneath to help guide the knife blade.

Removing the skin is easiest on a whole salmon fillet. Set the fillet on the work surface, skin-side down, so that the tail end is near you and the head end is pointing outward at about a 45-degree angle, toward your right side if you are right-handed, otherwise toward your left side. With a thin-bladed, sharp knife in one hand, hold the tip of the tail end of the fish securely against the work surface with the fingers of your other hand. Make a shallow, downward cut just in front of your fingers. Just before the blade reaches the skin of the fish, turn the blade to a nearly horizontal level, almost parallel with the work surface but a bit more downward than upward (which helps avoid leaving too much flesh attached to the skin). With gentle strokes in a sort of back-and-forth sawing motion, move the knife blade between the skin and the flesh toward the broader head end. Holding the skin firmly down with your other hand as you go will help greatly, so the knife slides through while the flesh and skin stay more or less in place.

If you need to remove the skin from a smaller fillet piece, and that piece happens to be a tail portion, just follow the instructions as noted above for the whole fillet. Otherwise, it may be easier to set the piece of fish flesh-side down and slide the knife between the skin and flesh from that position. This is true, too, if in skinning a whole fillet piece you accidentally cut the skin completely away only halfway through the process. In many cases, even if you don't intend to eat the skin it is best to cook the fish with the skin on, as it is much easier to remove once cooked. Salmon steaks are typically not skinned before cooking.

There are small pin bones that run in a single line down the center of the fish. While they're easier to remove when the fish is cooked (they slide right out when tugged), it's still a good idea to remove the bones before cooking to avoid any mishaps and make things easier on your guests.

My favorite tool for removing pin bones is a small pair of needle-nose pliers, the everyday hardware store type. Some bones are more firmly set in the flesh than others, and the pliers help get a good firm grip on the tiny bones. The bones are set in the flesh at a slight angle and can be hard to see. Run your fingers down the length of the fish, from tail to head end, and you should feel the tips of the bones (note they don't run all the way to the tail end, only about two-thirds of the way). Grab firmly with the pliers (you can also use a large pair of tweezers) and gently tug at the bone. Sometimes a bone tip will break off and you'll need to dig a bit farther in to nab the bone. All else fails, do the best you can and just warn dinner guests that there may be a rogue bone or two still in the fish.

Cooking Salmon

One thing to keep in mind with all techniques for cooking salmon is that fish pieces of different sizes and thicknesses will need different cooking times. Recipes will generally address this issue with a broader range of cooking times than you might be used to, because a salmon fillet piece you purchase one week might be just ½ inch thick, another week it could be over 1¼ inches thick. When cooking salmon it's important to check visual cues rather than just relying on the clock to tell you when the fish is done.

Grilling is ideal for richer, fattier fish because the richness of the flesh stands up well to the intense, direct heat without drying out. Best here are king and sockeye, stellar specimens that benefit from the "less is more" approach to cooking. Other salmon that have less fat and softer texture will benefit from being grilled whole, rather than in steaks or fillet pieces, as the skin will help retain a maximum of moisture and hold the meat together during cooking.

Baking is a great all-around technique for salmon. Leaner fish benefit from being covered with foil during baking, to avoid drying out, while richer fish may be baked uncovered. The fish pieces may be baked quite simply, on a baking sheet with a touch of seasoning, or arranged in a baking dish with thinly sliced onions on top and a splash of white wine. Small salmon may be baked whole with tasty results.

Steaming is best for smaller pieces of salmon that will cook quickly and evenly. This technique is good for all types of salmon, particularly for leaner salmon types, as the moist heat doesn't risk drying the fish out as grilling or pan-frying might.

I love pan-frying for all salmon. This cooking method serves up a sort of double-duty effect, more developed flavor on the surface after browning, while the interior flesh remains tender and delectable. It's not the best, though, for very thick fillet portions as the surface may become overcooked and dry by the time the center is cooked to your taste.

Poaching is probably my least favorite technique for salmon, primarily for reasons of flavor. I watch as the pieces simmer gently in the water, which turns slightly cloudy, with small dots of fat that glisten on the surface of the water, and see it as deliciousness seeping from the fish as it cooks. Poaching whole fish is a classic technique, though few kitchens today stock the long, slender poacher needed for this undertaking. Leaner salmon benefit from the moist cooking method, though richer fish will maintain a maximum of flavor when poached.

Planking is a technique today used for everything from pork chops to portobello mushrooms, but salmon is the quintessential ingredient for a wood plank. Usually made of cedar or alder, baking planks are thick enough to withstand many uses, often with slender metal bars down the length to help avoid warping. The planks also feature a ridge to hold in cooking liquids and avoid oven spillage. Because wood isn't much of a heat conductor, baking times will take longer on a plank than on a metal or glass baking pan.

There are also planks made specifically with outdoor grilling in mind, smaller and thinner. The planks are soaked in water first to temper the effects of the hot grill fire, fish and other ingredients taking on a subtly sweet, woodsy aroma as they cook. Typically these planks only fare well for one use.

I differ from some other cooks in the way I approach the degree of cooking salmon. I don't approach it as if cooking beef, that is to say cooking to differing "taste" preferences such as rare or medium. For one thing, given the nature of fish versus meat, pinpointing the specific levels of cooking is trickier than with beef. The carryover heat has a bigger impact on quick-cooking fish by the time the diner sticks his or her fork in the salmon. In even very nice restaurants I've been told by the server, upon ordering a salmon dish, that "the chef cooks the salmon rare and would that be all right?" After requesting medium instead, I still get a piece of fish that's essentially well done anyway. I'm particularly leery of richer, fattier fish being undercooked, as the flesh then has something of a flabby quality to my taste. Leaner salmon such as chum or coho certainly benefits from a touch less cooking than a rich king, since overcooked they risk drying out and losing a good deal of their flavor.

In my recipes here, I speak of cooking the salmon generally "until it has a touch of translucence in the center of the thickest part." I guess that could equate to "medium-well" or so in beef terms, which by the time you dig your fork in should be mostly cooked through but still moist. Feel free to alter the cooking level to suit your own taste, though keep in mind that raw or undercooked salmon that has never been frozen shouldn't be eaten by people with compromised immune systems, as from chemotherapy or AIDS.

SALMON EVENTS AND EXCURSIONS

This listing is just a sampling of the many salmon events held throughout the Pacific Northwest region each year.

JUNE

Copper River Wild Salmon Festival, Cordova, Alaska

It's only natural the area that provides us with some of the most prized salmon on the West Coast—late spring's run of Copper River salmon—should host a festival in honor of the fish. Held the first or second weekend of June each year, the three-day festival includes salmon runs (from the king salmon marathon to the one-mile "chum run"), live music, a community seafood picnic, a salmon barbecue, and gourmet Copper River Nouveau dinner. For more information, contact the Cordova Chamber of Commerce at 907-424-7260 or www.cordovachamber.com.

JULY

Steveston Salmon Festival, Richmond, British Columbia

This festival, held on Canada Day (July 1) every year, is the largest one-day festival put on by a nonprofit organization in British Columbia, and possibly all of Canada. More than 70,000 people come for the parade, children's festival, craft fair, flower and garden show, Japanese cultural show, wild salmon barbecue (1,200 pounds of it in 2003!), midway, and rides. Local salmon fishermen put on a net-mending demonstration too. For more information call 604-718-8080.

World's Largest Salmon Barbecue, Fort Bragg, California

Held on the first Saturday of July each year as part of the community's Fourth of July festivities, this big barbecue features a menu of grilled salmon, green salad, corn on the cob, and garlic bread—an ideal summertime feast. Live music serenades diners while they dig in. Proceeds from the barbecue fun go to the Salmon Restoration Association, which works to promote restoration of wild salmon runs in Northern California. For more information, go to www.salmonrestoration.com.

AUGUST

Sawtooth Salmon Festival, Stanley, Idaho

This two-day event sponsored by Idaho Rivers United is usually held at the end of August. It features guided walks to the salmon spawning beds, talks on salmon and the nearby river systems, traditional Native dance by the Shoshone-Bannock tribe, live music, arts and crafts, and food. For more information call 208-343-7481.

SEPTEMBER

Salmon Festival, Port Alberni, British Columbia

Held on Labor Day weekend every year, this festival, in the self-proclaimed "Salmon Capital of the World," features plenty of food, including a salmon barbecue, live music, and entertainment for children. A fishing derby takes place in the Port Alberni inlet on Friday, Saturday, and Sunday, with prizes awarded for the biggest salmon caught each day, as well as one for the biggest salmon of the weekend. Festivities begin on the Friday night and continue through Sunday. For more information, go to www.avcoc.com or call 250-724-6535.

Salmon Homecoming, Seattle, Washington

A five-day event, usually held the second or third week of September, the Salmon Homecoming is a multicultural celebration of the salmon and its importance as a natural resource in the region. An alliance of government agencies, Native Americans, and local businesses holds the celebration on the downtown waterfront, which includes music, arts and crafts, food (including a salmon bake), and a fun run, as well as educational activities, special programs for schoolchildren, and an environmental fair. For more information, call 206-381-9063 or go to www.salmonhomecoming.com.

Buoy Ten Brewfest, near Astoria, Oregon

Named for the popular sportfishing area at the mouth of the Columbia River, Buoy Ten near Fort Stevens State Park, this festival grew out of the Silver Salmon Oktoberfest that used to be held in October. Now held on the third weekend of September, many highlights will be the same—chief among them the chance to buy salmon direct from the fishermen on their boats, plus barbecued salmon and other seafood to eat, live music, arts and crafts, and children's activities, including making fish prints, hosted by the Astoria Children's Museum. Oregon beers and wines will be on tap as well, a true Northwest celebration. For more information, call 800-875-6807, go to www.oldoregon.com, or e-mail lauriewillie@charterinternet.com.

Wenatchee River Salmon Festival, Leavenworth, Washington

Usually held the third weekend of September at the Leavenworth National Fish Hatchery, this environmental education festival is a four-day event celebrating the return of the wild Chinook salmon to the Wenatchee River. There are two special school days for students, and the weekend attracts thousands of visitors who come to learn about the significance of salmon to the region, visit a Native American encampment, eat, and get lost in the Salmon Maze. For more information, go to www.salmonfest.org, or call 509-548-6662 ext. 250.

OCTOBER

Issaquah Salmon Days, Issaquah, Washington

This two-day event is an annual celebration, first held in 1970, to celebrate the return of the salmon to local streams and the downtown hatchery. Every year on the first full weekend in October, this festival, with its hundreds of artists, food vendors, live entertainment, children's activities, 5k and 10k runs, and tours of the hatchery, draws thousands of people to downtown Issaquah. For more information, go to www.salmondays.org or call 425-392-0661.

Oxbow Park Salmon Festival, near Gresham, Oregon

Held the second week of October each year in the Oxbow Regional Park, this two-day event that began as a "Salmon Appreciation Day" celebrates the return of Chinook salmon to the Sandy River. There are guided salmon viewing walks, musicians, storytellers, activities for children, educational displays, arts and crafts, wagon rides, and a salmon barbecue. For more information, call 503-797-1850 or go to www.metro-region.org/article.cfm?ArticleID=616.

YEAR-ROUND

Tillicum Village, Blake Island, Washington

A quick one-hour boat ride from Seattle's waterfront takes you to the shores of Blake Island where Northwest Coast Indians prepare a salmon feast for guests. Cultural dances and storytelling, as well as free time to explore the island's state park, are included in the trip. The lovely Puget Sound cruise is an added bonus. Some might call it a touristy outing, but it is one of a kind nonetheless and a great reminder of local Native traditions! Summer months offer multiple daily sailings, with a much lighter schedule come winter and early spring. For more information, go to www.tillicumvillage.com or call 800-426-1205.

Salmon Hatchery Celebrations, British Columbia

In April, May, and June, there are salmon send-offs from hatcheries all over British Columbia, and then more celebrations in August, September, and October when the fish return. For a list of hatcheries and celebrations, go to www3.telus.net/driftwood/festival.htm.

BUYING SALMON DIRECT

Something of a fish version of the farmers market, direct-sales opportunities across the Northwest allow consumers to go to the source and purchase salmon (and other seafood) direct from the fishermen who caught them. It's a great way to not only get top-quality fish, often freshly caught (otherwise frozen-at-sea), but also to learn more about how and where the fish was caught, and you can ask the fishermen for handling and cooking tips. This is just a sampling of such opportunities in our region:

Pillar Point Harbor
One Johnson Pier
Half Moon Bay, California

Fish sales hotline (updated daily): 650-726-8724
Troll-caught king salmon is available pretty consistently from May 1 through October, along with other seafoods throughout the year, including albacore tuna, rock fish, halibut, and Dungeness crab.

Fishermen's Terminal
West Wall, 4005 20th Avenue West
Seattle, Washington

General information: 206-728-3395
Most boats based at Fishermen's Terminal spend summers fishing up in Alaska so typically aren't on hand for direct sales May into September. The rest of the year, you can buy salmon, halibut, maybe spot prawns (most of the seafood will be flash-frozen) direct from the boats.

Columbia River Inter-Tribal Fish Commission
www.critfc.org

Recorded message: 888-289-1855
At multiple locations along the Columbia River—both the Washington and Oregon sides—from Cascade Locks to The Dalles, you can buy salmon and other fish (shad, steelhead) direct from Native fishermen.

In British Columbia, many coastal fishing towns have a government dock where salmon and other fish are sold directly from the boats. In the Vancouver area, you can find such shopping opportunities at False Creek, Granville Island, and in Steveston (at the mouth of the Fraser River). On Vancouver Island, notable options include Sydney, Ladysmith, Nanaimo, Port Alberni, Tofino, Campbell River, and Port Hardy. The buying opportunities and hours may be somewhat unpredictable, but keep an eye out for simple signs announcing sales that day, or head right to the harbor to see what kind of activity there is.

SALMON ONLINE

If this cookbook has whetted your appetite and you'd like to learn more about salmon in the Pacific Northwest, check out these online resources:

www.alaskaseafood.org
The Alaska Seafood Marketing Institute provides a good deal of consumer information on their Web site, relating to species, fishing methods, recipes, and health benefits for salmon as well as other seafoods harvested in Alaska.

www.bcsalmon.ca
Salmon information, recipes, harvest reports, and other information are available on this site from the British Columbia Salmon Marketing Council.

www.calkingsalmon.org
This site for the California Salmon Council includes a consumer section with recipes as well as contact information for suppliers of California troll-caught king salmon.

www.critfc.org
The Columbia River Inter-Tribal Fish Commission site provides information on the history of fishing on the Columbia River, information on the Native tribes involved, and buying information.

www.lummiislandwild.com
This site contains information on the reef-net salmon caught off Lummi Island as well as the chance to buy salmon (frozen in 50-pound boxes). Consider forming a buying club with friends or neighbors to make the most of this distinctive regional salmon.

www.msc.org
The Marine Stewardship Council is an independent nonprofit organization that promotes responsible fishing practices. On the site you can learn more about their certification program, including Alaska salmon, as well as recipes and other general seafood information.

www.oregonsalmon.org
The Oregon Salmon Commission Web site is more geared toward industry than consumers, though there is some general information about the salmon caught in the state, where to find them, and how to prepare them.

INDEX